OVERCOMING the Achievement Gap TRAP

Liberating Mindsets to Effect Change

Anthony Muhammad

Solution Tree | Press
a division of
Solution Tree

555 North Morton Street
Bloomington, IN 47404
800.733.6786 (toll free) / 812.336.7700
FAX: 812.336.7790
email: info@solution-tree.com
solution-tree.com

Visit **go.solution-tree.com/leadership** to download the reproducibles in this book.

Printed in the United States of America

19   18   17   8   9   10

Library of Congress Cataloging-in-Publication Data

Muhammad, Anthony.

  Overcoming the achievement gap trap : liberating mindsets to effect change / by Anthony Muhammad.

     pages cm

  Includes bibliographical references and index.

  ISBN 978-1-936763-27-6 (perfect bound) 1. Educational equalization. 2. Academic achievement--Social aspects. I. Title.

  LC213.2.M84 2015

  379.2'6--dc23

                     2015016018

Solution Tree
Jeffrey C. Jones, CEO
Edmund M. Ackerman, President

Solution Tree Press
President: Douglas M. Rife
Associate Acquisitions Editor: Kari Gillesse
Editorial Director: Lesley Bolton
Managing Production Editor: Caroline Weiss
Production Editor: Tara Perkins
Copy Editor: Sarah Payne-Mills
Proofreader: Elisabeth Abrams
Text and Cover Designer: Rian Anderson
Compositor: Abigail Bowen

This book is dedicated to my grandmother and mother. My grandmother, Emma L. Roberson-Alexander, departed this world on July 25, 2012, due to complications from diabetes. She was the rock of our family and provided the perfect blend of strength and compassion, so that all of us affected by her love could grow to become good people. I would also like to thank my mother, Anna V. Harper-Nelson, for taking good care of my grandmother during her period of failing health. Her strength, patience, and courage were awe-inspiring. These two women made me the man I am today, and for this reason, I dedicate this book to them.

Acknowledgments

Solution Tree Press would like to thank the following reviewers:

Leigh T. Barton
Assistant Professor,
  Educational Leadership
California State University,
  Fullerton
Fullerton, California

Sam Carter
Principal
Robinson Elementary School
Beloit, Wisconsin

Lena Christiansen
Principal
Dayton's Bluff Achievement
  Plus Elementary
St. Paul, Minnesota

Netty Hull
Assistant Professor of
  Education
Heritage University
Toppenish, Washington

Louis Lim
Vice Principal
Bayview Secondary School
Richmond Hill, Ontario,
  Canada

Richard J. Noblett
Principal
Olive Middle School
Baldwin Park, California

Michael C. Rodriguez
Professor, Quantitative
  Methods in Education
Campbell Leadership Chair
  in Education and Human
  Development
University of Minnesota
Minneapolis, Minnesota

Kim Spychalla
Principal
MacArthur Elementary
  School
Green Bay, Wisconsin

Christopher Wooleyhand
Principal
Richard Henry Lee
  Elementary School
Glen Burnie, Maryland

Visit **go.solution-tree.com/leadership** to download the reproducibles in this book.

Table of Contents

About the Author

 **Anthony Muhammad, PhD,** is a much sought-after educational consultant. A practitioner for nearly twenty years, he has servedas a middle school teacher, assistant principal, and principal and as a high school principal. His Transforming School Culture approach explores the root causes of staff resistance to change.

Anthony's tenure as a practitioner has earned him several awards as both a teacher and a principal. His most notable accomplishment came as principal of Levey Middle School in Southfield, Michigan, a National School of Excellence, where student proficiency on state assessments more than doubled in five years. Anthony and the staff at Levey used the Professional Learning Communities at Work™ process for school improvement, and they have been recognized in several videos and articles as a model high-performing PLC.

As a researcher, Anthony has published articles in several publications in both the United States and Canada. He is author of *Transforming School Culture: How to Overcome Staff Division* and *The Will to Lead, the Skill to Teach: Transforming Schools at Every Level* and a contributor to *The Collaborative Administrator*.

To learn more about Anthony's work, visit www.newfrontier21 .com, or follow him on Twitter @newfrontier21.

To book Anthony Muhammad for professional development, contact pd@solution-tree.com.

Preface

This is the book I always wanted to write. It is the culmination of the work I have done thus far as a practitioner, researcher, consultant, and author. I became an educator because I felt that it was the best way to combat inequality, and I wanted to live in a world where everyone had a fair shot at living his or her dream. So, I started my journey as a classroom teacher, and I loved the experience, but I felt limited in my ability to have influence on a broader scale, since I was restricted to the same 150 students every day. My next adventure was in school administration. I believed that platform would allow me the opportunity to shape an entire institution with my ideas and prove, beyond a shadow of a doubt, that equity could be achieved. I enjoyed that ride for a little more than a decade, and then I discovered that consulting and publishing would provide me with an even broader platform to not just influence one institution but thousands of institutions.

My goal as an author is to shape minds and help create institutions that embrace and achieve high levels of learning for all students. Before pursuing that goal, I believe that school systems and our entire society need to answer a major question: "Is equality even possible?" This question is essential to address in the struggle to achieve educational equality in schools. Benjamin Bloom (1981), a preeminent educational researcher in American history, states:

> After forty years of intensive research on school learning in the United States as well as abroad, my major conclusion is: What any person in the world can learn,

almost all persons can learn, if provided with the appropriate prior and current conditions of learning. (p. 137)

Bloom (1981) notes that this conclusion does not extend to people with severe cognitive disability or dysfunction, which he identifies as 1 to 3 percent of the population, but it is applicable to the other 97 to 99 percent if they are provided with the right conditions and enough time. Since Bloom's research, Robert Marzano (2003), who is often recognized as one of the greatest contemporary educational researchers in the world, concludes that we know enough to close every measurable achievement gap if schools would only seek and utilize the proven strategies. This is clear evidence that when a school is effective, uses the right methods, and creates the right conditions, it is able to develop high-level academic skills in nearly all of its students. So, if learning for all is possible, why do we have an achievement gap?

As I ventured into school consulting, I assumed that schools struggled with equal achievement outcomes because they did not have access to the right strategies and they did not have a system that would allow them to use the right strategies. In the early stages of my journey as a consultant, I found myself championing the Professional Learning Communities at Work™ model. I believed (and still do) that this model, which emphasizes professional collaboration and an intense focus on learning for all students, was the optimal method for delivering quality and equitable services for all students, and I spoke about that topic all over North America.

When a school accepts the challenge to become a professional learning community (PLC), the staff make a fundamental commitment to ensure high levels of learning for *all* students (DuFour, DuFour, & Eaker, 2008). This model requires the institution and the educators that work within the institution to organize their talents and resources to collectively answer four critical questions (DuFour, DuFour, Eaker, & Many, 2010).

1. What do we want students to learn?
2. How do we know if students have learned?
3. How do we respond when students don't learn?
4. How do we respond when students have learned?

The concept sounds logical and simple. A PLC requires a commitment to an aligned and equitable set of learning targets, a system of common formative assessment, an organized and data-driven system of support for students who missed the learning targets, and a system of enrichment for students who are ready to approach learning at a deeper level. What I appreciate about the model is the fact that it is so concrete. Student *learning* is the ultimate goal of a school.

As I consulted with schools on PLC implementation, I observed that some schools were prepared to benefit from the method and others were not. What I discovered was that organizational culture was a quintessential factor in the success or failure of good professional practice. So, my work started to shift toward the development of organizational culture, which would create an environment for the implementation of good teaching practice. If a school's organizational culture was able to improve, surely people would use the best research-based practices with universal high achievement as their primary goal.

As I delved further into the work of consulting and presenting, I began to get somewhat discouraged in my efforts to influence educational equality. I would travel from city to city speaking to practitioners in an effort to champion learning equality and build cultures where all kids can thrive, yet it seemed like the harder I worked, the bigger the problem of inequality became. I felt like a voice crying in the wilderness, and I started to wonder whether anyone still cared. I often pondered, "Does my work even matter?" I struggled to figure out what to do with my voice and the platform that I had been granted. Then, a new direction began to emerge, and three different experiences occurred within a relatively short period of time, convincing me that I had to write this book.

The Conference Call

Consulting has kept me busy. Each year, I spend more than two hundred days traveling and training educators. Typically, before I work with a school or school district, I have a conference call with the superintendent, curriculum leaders, and a few administrators to discuss the organization's needs, and they provide me with a little historical context to ensure that the day will result in a meaningful learning experience. Usually, these conference calls are pretty similar and not very memorable. But there was one conference call that left a lasting impression.

During the call, we were discussing the content for the day, and I raised the question, "Do you have any achievement gaps that you are concerned about?" The answer almost made me lose my breath. The superintendent answered, "We are working on the implementation of the Common Core State Standards. We don't have time to worry about achievement gaps!"

It was so surprising that I did not have a response. The person who is most responsible for ensuring equality and equity in her school district stated out loud that she did not have time for them. I did not realize that the climate of education had desensitized people to a point where equality and equity were not considered a pressing concern. I immediately felt compelled to shed light on this issue before it became totally forgotten and before young people came to believe that inequality is normal. There is a mindset developing within our school systems that undermines the importance of educational equality. Someone has to address it.

The Doctor's Visit

One afternoon, I was waiting with my wife in an exam room at the podiatrist's office. The doctor walked in after a short time, and before examining my wife's foot, he asked us a few personal questions. He asked me about my occupation, and I informed him that I was an educational consultant and I work with teachers and school leaders on school improvement and reform. He immediately gave us his entire philosophy about what's wrong with education and how it can be fixed. He said, "I volunteer and tutor kids from the Detroit Public Schools, and the biggest issue that I witness is *effort*. These kids just don't put in the effort. Nothing in life is achievable without effort. They have to care about school, and until they put in the effort, achievement will always be a problem."

Like with the school superintendent, I was speechless. A foot doctor felt qualified to summarize the problem with student achievement gaps in a rant only slightly longer than a *tweet*. All of the practitioners and scholars have apparently missed the mark, and a podiatrist has the answer? We can close achievement deficits if the kids who perform poorly just put in more effort? As I looked beyond the insulting nature of his opinion, which was unsolicited, I started to see the bigger picture. Not only is the achievement gap becoming a lower priority inside school systems, but private citizens are being convinced that the achievement gap is caused by some inherent flaw in the student (victim), not a systemic problem that could be fixed by improving professional practice. Somebody has to speak to this topic and give it a voice.

The Editorial

There is a routine in my house that occurs every Sunday morning without fail. My wife and I wake up and read the Sunday edition of the *Detroit Free Press*, and we enjoy a cup of coffee. April 13, 2014, was a little different than most Sundays because there was an editorial that caught my attention. The editorial "Why Michigan Is So Far Behind Others on Education" (Editorial Board, 2014) highlights an EdTrust report that documents Michigan's fall to the bottom half of the National Assessment of Educational Progress (NAEP), a test given annually to representative samples of students in grades 4, 8, and 12. The test is widely accepted as the most objective measure of student performance in mathematics and reading. The report notes that from 2003 to 2013, African American and Latino students in

Michigan have continued to lose ground on the NAEP test. As I read the article, the data did not surprise me, and the editorial appeared to be a typical diatribe about what's wrong with schools.

The second half of the editorial is what left me speechless again. The writers identified four reasons why Michigan students, especially minority students, lost ground from 2003 to 2013 compared to other states. They theorize that the decline in achievement is the result of four broad state actions during those years: (1) inconsistent state learning standards and curriculum, (2) an unwillingness to hold failing schools accountable and close poor-performing schools, (3) lack of teacher performance evaluation systems that encourage improvement with consequences for poor performers, and (4) inadequate and declining state funding for education.

A journalist felt qualified to sum up the entire problem with the decline in student performance in a two-page article. If the state would just set rigorous learning targets, students would perform better academically? It sounds simple to me. If we just close all the bad schools, students would perform better academically? It sounds simple to me. If we just use a tool that evaluates teacher effectiveness and keep the good teachers and fire the bad teachers, students would perform better academically? It sounds simple to me. If we just continue to throw more funding into systems that have not demonstrated a willingness or ability to effectively change, students would perform better academically? It's not that simple.

It sounds *too* simple, and years of research have taught us that all of those methods in isolation have no real effect on school performance and student achievement, as I will demonstrate in chapter 2. So, why are we beating this drum in 2015? Because it is politically expedient. The issue of educational equity has become a platform for lobbies that want to push a political and economic agenda. I will prove that many interested parties are using student test performance data to justify billions of dollars in expenditures that advance their political platform or line the pockets of those who become the beneficiaries of educational policy. This is a problem, and it needs to be voiced.

Introduction

*Education is the most powerful weapon which
you can use to change the world.*

—NELSON MANDELA

Since 2002, public education has been introduced to a whirlwind
of changes. We have experienced laws that mandate standardized testing and achievement levels for all public school students.
We have experienced a move toward aligning public school curric-
ula through adopting the Common Core State Standards (CCSS)
in English language arts and mathematics by forty-five states and
the District of Columbia (Academic Benchmarks, 2014). We also
experienced the Great Recession from 2007 to 2009, which resulted
in huge cuts to state and federal funding for education as well as a
massive decrease in home property values, which, in turn, led to a
decrease in property tax revenue that many school districts rely on
to fund their operations (Chakrabarti & Setren, 2011). Teacher evaluation rules are changing, and states are requiring a more detailed
process for evaluating teacher effectiveness, including value-added
analysis linked to student test scores. Labor rules are also changing,
and states like Michigan and Wisconsin have stripped away a lot
of the bargaining power that teacher unions enjoyed for decades
(Melchior, 2013). Educators have had their hands full with change

that is moving at a pace never seen before in the annals of public education.

So, why write a book about the achievement gap? My observations have led me to believe that all of the changes outlined here have served as a distraction from the critical problem in education: equality. Billions of dollars have been invested in creating student learning equality in public schools, but the data have shown us that this goal has not been reached. Inequality in achievement still exists along racial and economic lines. This issue of equality and fairness is built right into the core values of the United States, and all democratic nations, and I am not willing to allow the distraction of structural and political change to take the spotlight off an issue that still needs to be in the forefront of our collective social conscience.

Therefore, the purpose of this book is twofold. First, I want to establish that learning *equality* should be a professional and societal priority. We should not be able to predict student learning outcomes based on factors like income and race. Equality is the state of being equal, especially in status, rights, and opportunities. If we collectively answer the first critical question of a PLC, "What do we want students to learn?" there should be a universal expectation that all students who receive educational services related to those tangible learning targets should demonstrate a reasonable level of mastery of those skills. Politically, the cry for improvement in public schools has focused heavily on achieving learning equality, though the data do not show much growth in this area. In the following chapters, I will prove that inequality is a product of thinking that manifests itself in practice. Without examining our theories and thinking, focusing on policy and resource issues will do little to change the reality of learning inequality. We must embrace what I call the *liberation mindset* as we take on the hard work of changing the culture in schools to ensure all students, regardless of race, ethnicity, or level of affluence, are realizing their full potential.

The second major theme is *equity*. Equity is the quality of being fair and impartial. Former American Library Association president

Nancy Kranich (2001) writes, "In order to maximize opportunities for access experienced by certain groups, a good society commits resources, and develops a collective desire to level the playing field" (p. 15). Equity is important if we are going to achieve the goal of learning equality. We have to examine our professional practice and mindsets and ask if our traditional practices and belief systems have been fair to all students. My goal is to prove that fairness and impartiality have been missing from the experience of many struggling students, especially for poor and minority students, and that educational professionals and our society in general are perfectly comfortable with the achievement gap. Our society tends to embrace the idea of equality as a dogma, but society has not embraced the idea of equity in service and environment in order to achieve the equality that we claim we desire.

What This Book *Isn't*

I feel that it is important to be clear about the aim of this book before diving deeply into the core of the arguments. My experience has taught me that people tend to become defensive when their core values are challenged. Teacher expectations of student performance is a thorny issue in American education because of the inevitable overlay of accusations that low expectations for some groups of students reflect racial, ethnic, or class-based prejudice.

An Attempt to Devalue the Past

This book is not an attempt to devalue all the hard work and effort that many have contributed in the past to achieving academic equality. In fact, I will celebrate those efforts and build on the scholarship of the past. However, one painful reality has to be accepted: the achievement gap still exists, and it is nearly as wide as it has ever been. This fact has to compel those who sincerely want to close the gap to rethink past strategies and build on that foundation in our efforts to eliminate this stain on society once and for all.

An Attempt to Place Blame and Cause Division

Whenever someone ventures into the issues of race and class, he or she is often accused of being a troublemaker or placing blame. I do not believe it is fair to make this accusation of the people who dare attempt to hold a society accountable for the ideals and values that it claims to embrace. My colleague and coauthor of *The Will to Lead, the Skill to Teach: Transforming Schools at Every Level*, Sharroky Hollie, has coined the term *offensitive*, which means to be overly sensitive and easily offended. A society cannot explore complex issues if people are offensitive (Muhammad & Hollie, 2012).

In 1963, Martin Luther King Jr. says in his historic "I Have a Dream" speech in Washington, DC:

> In a sense we have come to our nation's capital to cash a check. When the architects of our republic wrote the magnificent words of the Constitution and the Declaration of Independence, they were signing a promissory note to which every American was to fall heir.
>
> This note was a promise that all men, yes, black men as well as white men, would be guaranteed the inalienable rights of life, liberty and the pursuit of happiness.
>
> It is obvious today that America has defaulted on this promissory note insofar as her citizens of color are concerned. Instead of honoring this sacred obligation, America has given the Negro people a bad check, a check which has come back marked "insufficient funds."
>
> But we refuse to believe that the bank of justice is bankrupt. We refuse to believe that there are insufficient funds in the great vaults of opportunity of this nation. So we have come to cash this check, a check that will give us upon demand the riches of freedom and the security of justice. (as cited in Lewis, n.d.)

Those sacred words summarize my sentiments perfectly. I do not feel uncomfortable producing facts and challenging others to reflect on the facts in relation to their own behavior. I did not create the achievement gap. I am one of many who are striving to close it. So, if a reader mistakes my passion for equality and the true pursuit of the American promise through the examination of facts, research, and historical truths for finger-pointing and blame, he or she has missed the entire point. If the reader is offensive, this will be a tough book to read. If the reader is truly concerned about the promise of equality, this book will feed your desire to pursue that goal.

An Extension of a Political Agenda

This book is not politically motivated. I am not pro-

- School choice
- Charter
- Accountability
- Privatization
- Integration

I am not anti-

- School choice
- Union
- Testing
- Common Core State Standards
- Segregation by choice

I am antidiscrimination, and I am pro-equality, and I am open to any method or resource that abolishes inequality and supports equality. I have no political party allegiances. As I will establish in chapter 1, both major political parties in the United States have to take responsibility for their contribution to the problem and their responsibility to help fix it. Both parties have passed legislation that has made the problem worse rather than better. My agenda is a human agenda, and that is my only allegiance.

What This Book *Is*

The achievement gap is a very complex issue, and I do not want the reader to think I am trying to oversimplify the problem like the editorial in the *Detroit Free Press* (Editorial Board, 2014) and offer a canned one-size-fits-all solution. My hope is to stir up a debate and invite people to think in ways that we have neglected in the past.

An Attempt to Rekindle and Resurrect the Issue of Equality

When I wrote the book *Transforming School Culture: How to Overcome Staff Division* in 2009, very few people were talking about the issue of organizational culture as it related to student achievement. I even had some people tell me that people were not interested in the topic and that I should focus my writing in more specific and vogue areas like curriculum, assessment, and instructional strategies. I chose to ignore conventional wisdom and tackle the topic, and the result was a best-selling book that made people talk about their behavior and their organizational culture in a candid way. The attention that book received made others start to examine the topic of school culture, and now it *is* a vogue topic, with many authors, practitioners, and thinkers focused on developing a healthy school culture. I did not think that one book would solve the dilemma of creating student-centered school cultures, but I believed that I could make a provocative case that would force people to take the topic seriously.

The achievement gap is the new area around which I would like to examine and reshape the thinking and conversation by introducing the concept of *mindset*. There have been many avenues explored in the pursuit of achieving equality in education, and all of them have merit, but perhaps the way that we have thought about this issue has been all wrong. I want to explore this topic and encourage people to examine it and talk about it.

A Challenge to the Status Quo

Not all students who attend public schools are succeeding, and that is not good. Activism is as American as apple pie. Nearly every gain made in American society came from activism. Women's voting rights, civil rights for minorities, and gay rights have all been the result of groups of people who challenged the status quo. They felt that discrimination should not be a disregarded stain on the societal landscape. These people chose to use their voices and influence to make a change. This book is a rallying cry for that type of activism.

The achievement gap has just become an accepted reality by adults inside and outside of the school. It seems to be as predictable as the morning sunrise, and there seems to be no sense of urgency to solve it. Author Don Miguel Ruiz (1997) refers to this dilemma as the *domestication of humans*, explaining:

> Through domestication we learn how to live and how to dream. The belief system that the domestication produces is like a Book of Law that rules our mind. Without question, whatever is in the Book of Law, is our truth. We base all of our judgments according to the Book of Law, even if these judgments go against our inner nature. (p. 9)

My instincts tell me that creating human hierarchies and differentiated levels of expectations is wrong. However, I also understand that it is very difficult to confront a domesticated society's beliefs and the Book of Law that governs its assumptions, behaviors, and actions.

Race (African American or black and Latino) and poverty are the two achievement gap factors that I will explore in this book. That does not discount the fact that other gaps exist, such as those based on gender or disability. This topic is too broad to champion every cause in one book, so we will examine the question, Why have *black*, *Latino*, and *poor* become synonymous with underachievement in school? This is an important question, and this book takes aim at a prevailing mentality that believes leaving these students behind is acceptable, and working to ensure their academic equality no longer matters.

A Call for Discomfort

When I was a student at Michigan State University, I attended school on an athletic scholarship. I was in tip-top shape, and youth, good genes, and a competitive spirit made my athletic feats feel almost effortless. But time has a way of making fitness more and more difficult. As I aged, competing athletically became a lot harder, and the things that once seemed natural and effortless became unnatural and took tremendous amounts of effort. Not only did competing against younger athletes become challenging, but just staying in basic shape was torturous!

The more comfortable I became with middle age, the more accustomed I was to being out of shape. By forty years of age, I was a shell of the world-class athlete I had been at nineteen years old, and I was really baffled by how easy it was to be OK with it. One day, I did not recognize the body of the person in the mirror. I made up my mind to make a change.

For motivation, I pulled out a picture of myself as a nineteen-year-old 400-meter champion. I was forty pounds heavier than the young athlete in the picture, so I began to do cardiovascular exercise and cut junk food out of my diet. In the beginning phases of my journey, I felt like giving up. It just hurt too badly! I experienced extreme muscle pain, joint irritation, and stiffness. But I kept looking at the picture, and I decided that the pain was worth it. Progress was slow, but I did not give up. I figured out that if the goal is important enough, I had to be willing to endure the pain of the transformation process. I made it through the pain, and I surpassed my goal. I now feel better physically and emotionally because I made up my mind to change my reality and to accept and conquer the pain in the process.

If the achievement gap is going to be closed, everyone involved in the process—educators, students, parents, and the greater society—have to experience growing pains. Those who have benefited from institutionalized privilege have to recognize their privilege and become advocates for social justice and change. In a society that prides itself on being fair and just, providing every child with a solid educational foundation should not be controversial. Superiority and equality cannot exist at the same time. Students, families, and schools who are at the bottom of the achievement gap have to reflect on their own perceptions and behaviors to try to improve their own station. Closing the achievement gap has to evolve from patronizing talk to real action and sacrifice by all parties.

A Voice for the Voiceless

This book is not motivated by sales or critical acclaim. Rather, it comes from a personal obligation I feel as a professional and as a citizen. I have been blessed with a platform and a voice, and I must speak on behalf of those who have not. I have sold thousands of books and spoken to hundreds of thousands of professionals. What good is that level of power and influence if I do not use it to promote the greater good?

It is a bold attempt to challenge society, and more importantly educational practitioners, and declare that all people matter. Poor people matter. People of every race and culture have value. Non-English speakers matter. Disabled people matter. Homeless people matter. All people matter, and a quality education is a right, not a privilege.

The Achievement Gap Trap

As American citizens, we tend to live between two polarized concepts: the image that we want to project and the reality where we are most comfortable residing. We love to claim concepts like equality, fairness, and justice as cornerstones of our core value system, while simultaneously living in a society that is not equal and not fair and just to all. In education, in the space between those two polarized realities lies a trap: the *achievement gap trap*. It is the zone between working to become an egalitarian school system and reaping the benefits of having a superior status to others or operating in a system with low expectations. Essentially, we know what to do, so why are we not doing what we know?

Stanford School of Business professors Jeffrey Pfeffer and Robert Sutton (2000) address this issue as it relates to progressive change in business with a concept that they call the *knowing-doing gap*. They pose the question: Why don't companies act on the knowledge that they've gathered? Instead of an *achievement gap trap*, they refer to the barrier as a *small talk trap*. People tend to ignore change that is potentially inconvenient and challenging in exchange for dogma and rhetoric that make them feel better. These authors suggest that real change leaders attach action to concepts and theories to move people out of their comfort zones, instead of tickling their ears with small talk (Pfeffer & Sutton, 2000). I assert that a similar dilemma exists in our society as it relates to educational equality and the difficult changes that it requires. It resonates with our souls conceptually, but I question the collective will to endure the discomfort necessary to make it a reality. In this book, I want to educate educators and community members about the comfort zone that we have created and conclude by attaching actions to the theories to actually create change.

Chapter Overviews

In this book, I will examine past theories, practices, and move-ments with a critical eye to determine what is still relevant and what needs to be left behind. I will seek to prove that the modern aca-demic achievement gap is more of a product of a prevailing *mindset* that perpetuates unequal learning outcomes as opposed to a product of factors such as funding, racial integration in schools, and pub-lic policy. The achievement gap has come to be seen as normal by schools and communities at the top and bottom of the academic achievement scale, and it will take a new culture and a new way of thinking to truly eliminate the glaring inequality that we witness in public education.

Chapter 1 examines the history of the achievement gap and cultural and societal factors that have contributed to its creation. Chapter 2 will establish the need to shift to a practical application of equality to embrace the promise of egalitarianism, rather than rewarding individual merit. Chapter 3 examines the need for a new framework to effect cultural change and identifies three mindsets that are at play in the struggle to effect this change: (1) the superiority mindset, (2) the victim mindset, and (3) the liberation mindset. To truly overcome the achievement gap trap, schools must embrace egalitarianism and the liberation mindset. Chapter 4 takes a close look at the superiority mindset. I will explore the psychological and material advantages of feeling superior to others and how schools play a major role in some communities' and citizens' need to feel superior. I will examine historical and current trends that prove that superiority complexes exist and that they have a real impact in school and in the greater society. Chapter 5 examines the victim mindset. I will answer the question: "Why would anyone want to be a victim?" This chapter will detail the psychological benefits to feeling powerless and holding others responsible for one's current station in life. This mindset is as culpable as the superiority mindset. Victims of discrimination and unfair systems have to take responsibility to be an active partner in their own ascension and demand change from the external system that perpetuates the inequality. Finally, chapter 6 proposes an alternative to the superiority and victim mindsets: the *liberation mindset*. The liberation mindset is rooted in three key principles: (1) equality, (2) responsibility, and (3) advocacy. I will provide case studies from three different schools that have embraced these concepts and the phenomenal improvements they have achieved as a result. This chapter will end with a set of surveys and diagnostic tools for any school to use to assess where it is on the liberation mindset journey.

Each chapter builds on the argument for a totally new approach to closing the achievement gap. The journey begins by looking in the mirror and accepting some painful facts. Then, there is a transition into exploring our thinking and our collective mindsets and their connection to the historically stratified student achievement results. Finally, I propose a new way of thinking that requires cooperation between educators, community members, and politicians that replaces the old thinking that created inequality with a liberating mindset that gives each student a fair opportunity to receive a world-class education regardless of personal circumstance.

CHAPTER 1

The Historical Context of the Achievement Gap

*You must maintain unwavering faith that you
can and will prevail in the end, regardless of the
difficulties,* AND *at the same time* have the
discipline to confront the most brutal facts about
your current reality, whatever they might be.

—*Jim Collins*

There are real measurable differences among the levels of educational benefit that various groups of students receive. These differences are popularly referred to as the *achievement gap*. Nearly all scholars, politicians, and professionals who are upset and moved to action about the achievement gap tend to focus heavily on the racial gap. Other than race, the second most discussed and analyzed factor affecting achievement inequality has been the issue of poverty.

Harvard University is a leading authority on this issue, and it has established the Harvard Achievement Gap Initiative (AGI), led by renowned scholar Ronald Ferguson. AGI is dedicated to the study and eradication of the achievement gap, which is defined as:

> the disparity in academic performance between groups
> of students. The achievement gap shows up in grades,
> standardized-test scores, course selection, dropout rates,
> and college-completion rates, among other success

> measures. It is most often used to describe the troubling
> performance gaps between African-American and
> Hispanic students, at the lower end of the performance
> scale, and their non-Hispanic white peers, and the similar
> academic disparity between students from low-income
> families and those who are better off. (Editorial Projects
> in Education Research Center, 2011)

A lot of time, money, and effort have gone into analyzing, dissecting, and fixing the achievement gap. I believe that most people who have been involved have been very sincere in their efforts, and they have provided great insight into the nature of the problem. However, the facts are crystal clear: the achievement gap has not closed.

The Facts

The U.S. Department of Education released a report in March 2014 that delivered somber news to those with hopes that efforts to close the achievement gap had produced tangible, positive results. The report, the *Civil Rights Data Collection* issue brief, includes findings from every public school in the United States, comprising about forty-nine million students. Following are some of the key findings (U.S. Department of Education, Office for Civil Rights, 2014).

- Among high schools serving the highest percentage of African American and Latino students, one in three do not offer a single chemistry course, and one in four do not offer a course more advanced than algebra 1.

- In schools that offer gifted and talented programs, African American and Latino students represent 40 percent of students, but only 26 percent of those enrolled in such programs.

- African American, Latino, and impoverished students attend schools with higher concentrations of first-year teachers than do white students.

- African American students are suspended and expelled from school at a rate more than three times as high as white students (16 percent versus 5 percent).

Student performance in mathematics and reading has always been an acceptable measure of student progress in school. Those most closely associated with the achievement gap have kept a close eye on trends surrounding these data. As previously noted, the NAEP, or Nation's Report Card, is widely accepted as the most objective measure of student performance in mathematics and reading, providing scholars, practitioners, and lawmakers with a broad picture of national education trends. The report has shown that over a twenty-year period, the academic growth of African American, Latino, and impoverished students has steadily increased. However, the gains are not significantly outpacing the growth of other student groups. NAEP results from 2013 reveal that the average score of African American and Latino students in fourth- and eighth-grade mathematics and reading compared to white students was more than twenty points lower, equivalent to more than two grade levels behind. The twelfth-grade scores reveal a gap of more than forty points in mathematics and reading, equivalent to more than four grade levels behind. This is popularly called the *four-year gap*, meaning that the average African American and Latino high school senior has mathematics and reading skills equivalent to the skills of an average white eighth grader (Lee, 2014).

Racial Inequalities

Race seems to be the most illogical factor regarding the achievement gap, and it strikes the heaviest emotional chord. It seems improbable that we should be able to predict the achievement of a group based on the level of pigmentation or melanin present in people's skin, but we have been able to track these data for decades. What makes this even more troubling is that race is deemed a *social construct*. A *social construct* is a mechanism, phenomenon, or category that develops meaning for individuals or groups through social practice (Herrnstein & Murray, 1994). Therefore, although a person's race (black, Latino, white, and so on) is genetic, people's ideas and perceptions of that race are socially constructed. In essence, race is only a figment of our imagination. It only has value in our minds and in our social systems. So, race cannot be the problem; the problem must be our *perception* about race and how race has played out in our society historically in a concept called *racism*. To illustrate this concept, consider how renowned African American 19th and 20th century philosopher W. E. B. Du Bois discusses how racism has affected both black and white members of American society by describing it as a *veil*, saying, "The Negro is a sort of Seventh son, born with a veil, and gifted with second sight in this American world" (Du Bois, 2008, p. 12). Author Mark Stafford (1989) explains that "the 'veil' was the fabric of racism that kept blacks concealed from whites, and it also kept blacks from seeing themselves clearly" (p. 57).

Racism is a belief or doctrine that inherent differences among the various human races determine cultural or individual achievement, and it usually involves the idea that one's own race is superior and has the right to rule others. It can manifest in policies, systems, or governments based on the same doctrine (Racism, n.d.). Black and Latino students are referenced most when it comes to the issue of the U.S. achievement gap. There are other students who perform poorly in school compared to whites, including Native American and Pacific Islander students, but these gaps do not receive as much attention as the black and Latino gaps, as these groups make up 1.2 percent and 0.2 percent, respectively, of the country's makeup, as compared to black (13.2 percent) and Latino (17.1 percent) (U.S. Census Bureau, 2014).

Ironically, Asian students outperform white students at every grade level of the NAEP in both mathematics and reading. So, why is there not an outcry for fixing the white-Asian achievement gap? Abigail Thernstrom and Stephan Thernstrom (2003) theorize that many of the important values of Western European culture and East Asian culture are similar. American schools value obedience, mastery of content, and personal commitment to excellence, which are not in conflict with East Asian values. In essence, according to Thernstrom and Thernstrom (2003), the similarity in values makes Asians an extension of the white value system rather than a threat to it.

Thus, our social view of race is a problem for both the perpetuator of racism and the victims of racism. In our journey to achieving equality in schools and closing the achievement gap, the first step is to acknowledge that racism exists. Without this first step, recovery is nearly impossible.

Public Opinion

In a society that publically states its commitment to equality, freedom, and liberty, it would seem logical to conclude that conditions and realities contrary to those foundational principles would appall most people. The assumption would be logical but not true. Polls show that the majority of U.S. citizens have unfavorable opinions of black and Latino citizens as well as impoverished citizens.

In 2008, America elected its first nonwhite president, Barack Obama. Although Obama is of mixed racial heritage (his mother is white, and his father is Kenyan), the greater American and international community celebrated the election of America's first black president. Many commentators claimed that Obama's election symbolized that the country had entered a postracial era. A University of Michigan study conflicts with those sentiments (Pasek, Krosnik, & Tompson, 2012). The study reports that Americans' unfavorable opinions of blacks actually increased between Obama's election in 2008 and his re-election campaign in 2012. According to the study, the American unfavorable rating of blacks in 2008 was 49.3 percent; by 2012, that number had grown to 55.7 percent. The study found that unlike any other president in American history, the opinion of the job performance of the president had an impact on many Americans' view of African Americans in general. The election of a black president coincided with a shift in American attitudes toward blacks, but in a negative fashion, challenging the notion that we live in a postracial era.

A 2013 study published in the *Hispanic Journal of Behavioral Sciences* finds that American attitudes about Latino citizens are not any better than those of blacks (Lyons, Coursey, & Kenworthy, 2013). The study shows that 54 percent of American citizens view Latinos negatively in general, but the unfavorable rating jumped to 77 percent for Latinos who were undocumented immigrants. The study finds that the majority of Americans polled felt that Latinos were a major contributor to crime and illegal activity and undocumented Latino immigrants should be deported. A 2012 poll by the National Hispanic Media Coalition and Latino Decisions finds that more than 30 percent of non-Latino Americans believe that the majority (more than 50 percent) of Latinos living in America are undocumented illegal aliens, but statistical data identify the number around 16 percent (Lilley, 2012). The researchers that initiated this poll conclude that media coverage of Latinos or Hispanics has led to a strong connection between the terms *Hispanic* and *illegal immigrant.*

Public apathy toward the poor follows similar lines. In the 1960s, President Lyndon Johnson launched his War on Poverty aimed at investing government resources to eliminate American poverty. American sentiment about poverty is very different in the 21st century. At the time of Johnson's efforts, 91 percent of Americans polled in 1965 believed that helping the poor was a top government priority (Connell, 1993). A Pew Research Center poll conducted in 2012 reveals that only 52 percent of Americans polled felt that helping the poor was a top priority (Pew Research Center for the People and the Press, 2012). The Pew poll also reveals that 62 percent of Americans felt that lack of personal responsibility and personal ambition were the primary reasons for modern poverty.

These studies and polls illustrate that the American public does not have a highly favorable opinion of black, Latino, and impoverished citizens. This might explain why the achievement gap has garnered so much apathy. People typically do not expect much from those that they do not view as favorable or capable, and educators are no exception. The personal perceptions and value systems of educators have a profound effect on student learning outcomes (Zeichner & Gore, n.d). The attitudes that we witness in school are a manifestation of a greater set of beliefs and attitudes that we witness in society. Based on the facts and figures provided in this section, it is hard to deny that racism does not exist in our society. Critical race theory can help us better understand this complex topic.

Critical Race Theory

Critical race theory (CRT) emerged in the 1970s when a group of legal and academic scholars came together to study the subtle nuances of the problems associated with race and equality in the United States. Multiple themes provide a foundation for CRT, including the following (Delgado & Stefancic, 2012).

- **Racism as a "normal" part of societal function:** Authors of *Critical Race Theory: An Introduction* (2012) Richard Delgado and Jean Stefancic describe this phenomenon as *normal science*, and because our society accepts it as ordinary, it is difficult to cure except for the most blatant forms of discrimination.

- **Interest convergence:** A large section of the American population has no vested interest in eradicating racism. Wealthy whites have a material interest in maintaining racism, and working-class whites have a psychological advantage to uphold.

- **Social construction thesis (as previously highlighted in this chapter):** Race is a product of social thought and relations. Its function is not a product of objective information or scientific fact; it is a product of social thinking.

Gloria Ladson-Billings has been a leader in the study of critical race theory in education, and she theorizes that the racial achievement gap is a by-product of a deeper battle for power, using race as its anchor. She and colleague William Tate identify this power as the power to construct, define, and control reality through the lens of white privilege (Ladson-Billings & Tate, 1995). They point out that schools are a part of a larger structure of institutionalized racism and without acknowledgment and collective action, the system will do what it was designed to do: perpetuate inequality.

I have established that there is substantial evidence to support the theory that our personal views are shaped by our life experiences, and those views have an impact on student achievement. This is particularly true when it comes to the issues of race and poverty. As Ladson-Billings and Tate (1995) explain, schools have become a part of a system that maintains inequality, and many educators do not even recognize they are partially culpable.

In an attempt to try and move the process of student academic equality forward, it is important to examine the events of the past. The true examination of past injustice should provide educators with some context for current inequalities and the systems and practices that maintain inequality. The purpose of acknowledgement is not to demonize or vilify. The intent is to bridge gaps in understanding and perceptions so that we can collectively find a common solution.

This is not a new concept. After the fall of the apartheid regime in South Africa in the 1990s, a system designed to overtly institutionalize racism through laws and lethal force, the new democratically elected government set up a Truth and Reconciliation Commission (TRC). The TRC was seen as a critical component of the nation's transition from a discriminatory past to a fair and all-inclusive future. Both the victims of past discrimination and the perpetuators were allowed an unedited voice that enabled them to purge, dialogue, and move beyond the pain of the past. By most accounts, the TRC was essential and prevented potentially violent and volatile clashes that could have torn the country apart if truthful dialogue about the impact of the past was not acknowledged (Cole, 2009). If there is no acknowledgement of the truth of the past, I do not see much hope for future reconciliation.

African Americans

Racism in the United States as it relates to black and white relationships has always been met with strong emotions. As the founding fathers of the United States were drafting the Declaration of Independence from Great Britain's rule, these same men lived in a society that legalized the enslavement of people of African descent, and many of these delegates owned slaves personally. The Independence Hall Association (www.ushistory.org), a well-respected historical society dedicated to preserving American history, describes the paradox of freedom and slavery at the signing of the Declaration of Independence as follows:

> Thomas Jefferson provides the classic example of the contradictions of the Revolutionary Era. Although he was the chief author of the Declaration, he also owned slaves, as did many of his fellow signers. They did not see full human equality as a positive social goal. Nevertheless, Jefferson was prepared to criticize slavery much more directly than most of his colleagues. His original draft of the Declaration included a long passage that condemned King George for allowing the slave trade to flourish. This implied criticism of slavery—a central institution in early American society—was deleted by a vote of the CONTINENTAL CONGRESS before the delegates signed the Declaration. (Independence Hall Association, n.d.)

Of the fifty-six delegates that signed the Declaration of Independence, one-third to one-half owned slaves. Most notably among them are Thomas Jefferson, who was the creator of the equality phrase "We hold these truths to be self-evident, that all men are created equal"; George Washington, who became the nation's first president; and Patrick Henry, who is most noted for the quote, "Give me liberty, or give me death."

The institution of chattel slavery was legal in the United States from 1619 to 1865. During those 246 years, movements fought to eliminate this institution. One of these was the abolitionist movement, of which many notable signers of the Declaration of

Independence were active members, including Alexander Hamilton, John Jay, John Adams, Samuel Adams, and Thomas Paine (Pavao, 2014). The abolitionist movement provided some relief to the millions of enslaved blacks in America, but the conflict ended with the American Civil War, the bloody battle between the northern and southern members of the Republic. According to the esteemed African American history scholar Henry Louis Gates Jr. (2014), at the end of the Civil War, there were more than four million blacks serving as slaves in the American south that were set free and placed into a society where they had been slaves for almost 250 years.

The journey of African Americans and racism did not stop with the abolition of slavery. Racism continued through legalized discrimination known as the Jim Crow laws from 1877–1964. Named after a 19th century minstrel song and dance stereotyping African Americans, Jim Crow affected the lives of millions of people. It came to personify the system of government-sanctioned racial oppression and segregation in the United States after the Civil War (King, 1995).

Jim Crow laws included the legal separation of the races into separate classes with whites being the privileged and blacks being the less privileged. Jim Crow segregation created a caste system, separating things as simple as access to toilets and water fountains and as complex as housing access, voting rights, public education, and even legal lynching. The United States federal government upheld these laws until President Lyndon Johnson signed the Civil Rights Act of 1964, declaring this system of segregation illegal. The system was outlawed, but the Civil Rights Act could not erase the psychological damage from eighty-seven years' worth of legally enforced inferiority.

The modern era of racism is not as overt as physical enslavement or legal separation and discrimination. The modern era brings about a tragedy that is even worse, because it is less overt and possibly explained by factors more internal than external. Michelle Alexander (2012) best describes this new form of racism in her

Pulitzer Prize–winning book *The New Jim Crow: Mass Incarceration in the Age of Colorblindness.* In this book, she asserts that Ronald Reagan's War on Drugs, launched in 1982, introduced a new era of institutionalized racism known as mass incarceration. She asserts that "we have not ended racial caste in America; we have merely redesigned it" (p. 2).

This initiative was sold to the American public as a sincere effort to rid communities of drug use, abuse, and crime. Ironically, drug use was on the decline at the time this initiative was launched, and less than 2 percent of American citizens viewed drugs as a serious national issue (Roberts & Hough, 2002). In 1982, there were just over 300,000 Americans serving prison sentences, and that number has ballooned to over 2.5 million, with drug-related convictions as the single largest factor responsible for the drastic increase (Mauer, 2006). Though illegal drug use and distribution rates are similar among all races (Ingraham, 2014), blacks have been convicted for drug use or distribution disproportionately compared to other races. African Americans are convicted of drug crimes fifteen times more often than white Americans (Office of Applied Studies, Substance Abuse and Mental Health Services Administration, 2001). The War on Drugs pushed lawmakers to pass mandatory minimum sentences for drug offenses (such as a minimum of five years imprisonment for possession [Alexander, 2012]), which were much more draconian than the sentencing requirements for other crimes. A prosecutor and a judge do not have much wiggle room for lenient sentences when drug charges carry such a heavy sentencing weight. In 2014, U.S. Attorney General Eric Holder and Kentucky Senator Rand Paul made this issue of mandatory minimum sentencing and its disproportionate effect on African Americans a legislative priority, and they are fighting to have these laws repealed (Apuzzo, 2014).

Alexander (2012) points out that in cities like Detroit and Chicago, as many as 80 percent of young African American men have a criminal drug offense on their records, and more than 75 percent are for minor offenses like misdemeanor possession. This drug record can follow them for the rest of their lives, and these men become permanent fixtures in the criminal justice system, which may prevent them from qualifying for many high-paying jobs, impact their potential for college admission and federal financial aid, and even restrict their driving and voting privileges. In essence, the current system of racism is a combination of enslavement and Jim Crow.

In addition to federal drug laws and policies that disproportionately affect the African American community, self- and community hate has become a prevalent fixture in the African American community. During the civil rights movement of the 1950s and 1960s, popular culture supported the fight for equality. Songs like "Fight the Power" by the Isley Brothers and "Say It Loud—I'm Black and I'm Proud" by James Brown helped fuel an era of racial pride in the African American community. Today, that same community is bombarded with music and screen images that perpetuate self-hate and a misogynistic mentality.

Popular recording artists like Lil Wayne and Rick Ross are flooding the airwaves, and consequently the minds of people around the world, with songs full of profanity, glorified illegal drug use and commerce, blatant materialism, the objectification of women, and sexual promiscuity. These messages also carry over into television and movies. African American television shows like *The Cosby Show* of the 1980s and 1990s, which reinforced the power of education, family life, and positive integration into American society have been replaced with reality shows like *Basketball Wives*, *The Real Housewives of Atlanta*, and the blockbuster Fox drama *Empire*, which chronicles the lives of colorful African American characters that build a record empire with drug money. These shows help create a societal narrative that depict African Americans as savage and incapable of self-control and basic human decency.

Travis Lars Gosa (2008), assistant professor of social science at Cornell University, best describes the effect that the emergence of this subculture has had on African American youth, especially as it pertains to the pursuit of an education:

> I find that hip-hop's dominant folk theory of achievement holds that black youth who lack athletic and rhyme skills *must* pursue drugs and street crime. According to many of the lyrics, "people like us" have only three viable routes to success: drugs, sports, and hip-hop. This vision of the opportunity structure reinforces claims that education does not lead to success in the adult labor market and helps rationalize the decision to abandon academic achievement. Street stories contribute to an image of economic success that cannot be reasonably obtained through education or legal means. (p. 120)

In his book *Brainwashed: Challenging the Myth of Black Inferiority*, Tom Burrell (2010), founder of the multicultural advertising agency Burrell Communications Group, writes:

> African Americans, no matter how savvy, educated, or financially privileged, could not completely avoid the conditioning that resulted from increasingly sophisticated bombardment of subtle and not-so-subtle messages created to reinforce how different and inherently inferior blacks are compared to whites. (p. 5)

Racism against African Americans has evolved over the last four hundred years. It began as a form of physical and psychological enslavement at the hands of a white and overtly racist slave master. The system of physical bondage changed to a system of legal segregation that reinforced the white race's superiority and the black race's inferiority. The mechanism then morphed into a criminal justice system that disproportionately prosecutes and incarcerates African Americans for drug crimes, especially petty drug charges, that has led to mass incarceration and a lifetime of disadvantage because of criminal history. Finally, it has reared its head in the ugliest form of self-hatred in popular culture, where music artists condition African Americans and the world to view the race as a subculture unworthy of respect and dignity. If we are serious about closing the achievement gap, we have to acknowledge these facts.

Latinos and Hispanics

The other races synonymous with the term *achievement gap* are Latinos or Hispanics. There is even a controversy over the terminology used to describe this group. Is it *Latino* or *Hispanic*? For the purpose of this book, I will use both terms interchangeably, but Kimberly Simmons, the director of Latin American Studies at the University of South Carolina, says:

> For self-identification, there's more of a movement and a shift to say *Latino* in the United States. *Latino* has become a way to unify the different groups in Latin America, the children of those who are here from different countries, under a larger umbrella. *Latino* has become the new politically correct term. (Austin & Johnson, 2012)

The grouping of people under *Hispanic* or *Latino* did not emerge until the U.S. census of 1970. The terms embrace roughly two dozen national-origin groups that have little in common beyond the fact that they originated in countries in the Western Hemisphere that at one time were a part of the Spanish empire and have remained Spanish speaking. Puerto Ricans, Dominicans, Ecuadorians, and Cubans are all very different in their cultural heritage and history. The study *The Hispanic Population of the United States* on the 1980 census indicates, "It is impossible to speak of a single, unified 'Hispanic population' in any strict sense of the term" (Bean & Tienda, 1987, p. 398). Even though the facts tell us that it is very difficult to define this wide variety of individuals and cultures from all around the Western Hemisphere, we still refer to them using one broad term and categorization. The 2010 U.S. census calculated the Hispanic population as 50.5 million, and at that point it was the single fastest-growing ethnic group in the United States. In 2014, the population numbered just over 53 million (Passel, Cohn, & Lopez, 2011).

According to the U.S. Census Bureau (2014), almost two-thirds of the Latinos living in the United States are from Mexico. In turn, many of the characteristics, stereotypes, and assumptions associated with the terms *Latino* or *Hispanic* become synonymous with *Mexican*. Data and figures for the Hispanic population in general will at least be reasonable estimates of what is true for Mexican Americans because the group is so large that it dominates the averages (Therrien & Ramirez, 2001). The majority of the Mexican population is concentrated in the southwest portion of the United States in states like Arizona, California, Texas, and New Mexico, though population rates are growing rapidly all across the United States in places like Tennessee and Illinois. Only 36 percent of the 5.4 million legal Mexican immigrants choose a path to citizenship, and nearly 60 percent speak Spanish as a first language (Gonzalez-Barrera, Lopez, Passel, & Taylor, 2013; Pew Hispanic Center, 2002).

Unlike African Americans, the history of racism associated with Latinos does not involve enslavement or overt and legal systems of segregation. The three major areas of racism leveraged on Latinos are associated with immigration status, indigenous culture, and English language acquisition. No state has had more experience with these three forms of racism than the state of Arizona.

On April 23, 2010, Governor Jan Brewer of Arizona signed the Support Our Law Enforcement and Safe Neighborhoods Act. The law enforces state requirements and penalties related to immigration laws, with provisions for trespassing, the harboring and transportation of illegal immigrants, alien registration documents, employer sanctions, and human smuggling (Morse, 2011). This law set off a heated political debate, especially among the Latino community because of a provision for reasonable suspicion. This provision empowers law enforcement officers, when in the context of enforcing the law, to ask for proof of immigration status from any detainee that they deem "reasonably suspicious." In a country that is made up of races and nationalities from every corner of the globe, how can a law enforcement officer determine who is potentially an illegal immigrant? The Latino community feared that having brown skin and speaking Spanish constituted reasonable suspicion. Roberto Rodriguez (2012), an assistant professor of Mexican American studies at the University of Arizona, writes:

> Law enforcement officials are convinced that this provision cannot be implemented without racial profiling. Throughout the country, when one invokes the concept of reasonable suspicion in the context of immigration enforcement, chances are that brown skin and the use of the Spanish language comes to mind.

In 2010, Arizona also passed Senate Bill 2281, which prevents schools from establishing courses or programs that:

- Promote the overthrow of U.S. government
- Promote resentment toward any race or class
- Are designed for a certain ethnicity
- Advocate ethnic solidarity instead of individuality

Critics of the law say that it was specifically aimed at Tucson Unified School District's Mexican American studies curriculum (Calefati, 2010; Planas, 2013). Some Arizona lawmakers felt that the courses did not support Mexican student assimilation into mainstream American values and that the curriculum promoted the alienation of American culture in language in exchange for the indigenous Mexican culture and Spanish language. State Superintendent Tom Horne first introduced the bill, which State Superintendent John Huppenthal spearheaded once Horne became attorney general. Once it passed, Tucson Unified School District was found in violation of the law and was threatened with a 10 percent loss of state funding ($14 million) if the Mexican American studies classes continued. In regard to the ruling, Federal Judge Wallace Tashima, says, "This single-minded focus on terminating the MAS (Mexican-American Studies) program, along with Horne's decision not to issue findings against other ethnic studies programs, is at least suggestive of discriminatory intent" (Planas, 2013). Attorney Richard Martinez filed an appeal on behalf of the Tucson Unified School District. However, the U.S. Court of Appeals upheld the law.

An argument over language buttresses the racism associated with immigration status and culture: Americans speak English, and to live in the United States without being fully fluent in English is un-American. The history of immigration in the United States has always culminated with full integration into the society through English replacing the indigenous language. This was the case with the Polish, Italians, French, Germans, and all other non-English-speaking immigrants (Cummins, 2000). So, just like the previous matters, Arizona chose to create laws.

In 2000, Arizona mandated the structured English immersion (SEI) model after the passage of Proposition 203. With this proposition, public school districts and charter schools were required to use SEI for English learners (ELs) (Gándara & Orfield, 2010). The SEI also requires schools to group ELs based on their English language proficiency and set a specific number of minutes for each component of language instruction (Garcia, Lawton, & de Figueiredo, 2010). Additionally, the Arizona English Language Learners Task Force implemented the four-hour English language development block model (Mahoney, MacSwan, Haladyna, & Garcia, 2010). The four-hour block model requires ELs to receive English language development services in an English-only immersion setting for a minimum of four hours per day for the first year they are classified as an EL. This regulation is based on an assumption that ELs can achieve proficiency in English very quickly (usually within a year) in an English-only instructional environment. To exit the mandatory four-hour block model, ELs must master English at their grade level on the state's English language proficiency test, the Arizona English Language and Literacy Assessment (Garcia et al., 2010).

A model featuring prolonged daily segregation and the grouping of students by language proficiency does not align with research in the field of second-language acquisition or cognitive infrastructure theories associated with the development of second-language learners (August, Goldenberg, & Rueda, 2010). EL students in Arizona have not produced huge gains in English acquisition based on these policies. In fact, the gap between Arizona ELs and EL students in other states has grown steadily since adopting the Proposition 203 provisions, and state lawmakers refuse to take a different course even though the data clearly indicate that this course of action has not been successful (Garcia et al., 2010).

There are, of course, barriers for Latinos outside of educators' direct control that create a climate of failure. Tensions over issues like immigration status, native culture, and English language acquisition help create a social theory that something is inherently wrong with Latino students, and consequently, we expect less of them. Racism exists, and it is at the core of why we have a racial achievement gap in the United States.

Income Inequality and Poverty

Unlike the socially constructed term *race*, poverty is real, and the lack of resources affects every aspect of life for those suffering from it. In fact, the topic of income inequality has been in the news frequently and was a major talking point of the Obama administration in 2013 (Kuhnhenn, 2013). The lack of access to quality food and health care can negatively affect a child at a physiological level. The lack of income can also affect a child intellectually. The lack of financial means can deprive students from experiencing travel and other cultural experiences which provide context for academics. Poverty can also deny a child's access to varieties of literature and technology. In fact, poverty is one of the most debilitating disadvantages students can have as they begin their academic journey (Hattie, 2009).

Poverty by the Numbers

The poverty rate has historically fluctuated as the result of periods of economic prosperity and recession, with the 2013 trend resulting from the Great Recession starting in 2007. The U.S. Census Bureau tracks these numbers, and the results are not good (DeNavas-Walt, Proctor, & Smith, 2013).

- 46.5 million people (15 percent) earn incomes below the national poverty line, up from 11.3 percent in 2000.
- 30.4 million adults (22.8 percent) and 16.1 million American children (21.8 percent) live in poverty.
- 9.5 million (11.8 percent) families live in poverty.

As more American citizens find themselves living below the national poverty line, this trend also shows that people are not feeling the pain equally. When adjusted for inflation, household income has declined for the average family since 1999. Elise Gould, an economist at the Economic Policy Institute, says:

> This long-term decline in income is troubling to economists, especially as the middle and lower classes have fared considerably worse than the rich. Since 1967, Americans right in the middle of the income curve have seen their earnings rise 19%, while those in the top 5% have seen a 67% gain. Rising inequality is seldom a sign of good social stability. (as cited in Hargreaves, 2013)

Gould also points out that the income pain is not evenly distributed from a racial perspective. In 2012, Asians had the highest median household income ($68,636), followed by whites ($57,009), Hispanics ($39,005), and blacks ($33,321). Women also fared very poorly when compared to men, earning only 77 percent of what men made (DeNavas-Walt et al., 2013).

Poverty and the Achievement Gap

Like race, there has yet to be substantive acceptance that poverty is a social ill and that it is everyone's problem. In a meritocracy, people earn their place, and their life is a testament to their personal commitment and achievement or lack thereof. However, economists Samuel Bowles and Herbert Gintis (1976, 2011) argue that in the United States, parents' economic status, rather than achievement, is the best predictor of their children's economic status. Furthermore, they argue that schools are institutions that prepare students for the workplace through hierarchical relationships to maintain the current distribution of wealth and economic power structure (Bowles & Gintis, 1976, 2011). Even if those types of sociological theories are too far-fetched for some, the evidence is clear: students who are raised in homes where the income level is low are likely to suffer in school and tend to stay in poverty into adulthood.

The 2012 report *Concentration of Poverty in the New Millennium* (Jargowsky, 2013) discusses 20th century and 21st century poverty trends and the impact on high-poverty neighborhoods and schools. The report shows that since the U.S. census in 2000, poverty deviated from its traditional pattern of rural and inner-city concentration. The fastest-growing poverty areas are in suburban areas and traditionally stable small-town areas where an industry once flourished. The shift is now affecting students of all races and backgrounds, and school districts are asked to address needs that they have historically never had to address like hunger, basic health services, and basic academic skills that prepare children for success in kindergarten. Not only are more schools being pressed to meet students' basic needs at a rate never seen before, but the neediest schools are attracting teachers and administrators with the lowest job qualifications. According to a 2006 report, schools with student poverty rates above 40 percent are attracting new teachers who, on average, achieve in the bottom third of their graduating classes. Additionally, their school leaders are more likely to see the school as a stepping stone to upward mobility, making their longevity rate nearly half that of principals who are assigned to schools with high levels of economic affluence (Clotfelter, Ladd, Vigdor, & Wheeler, 2006).

Unfortunately, the growth in U.S. poverty mostly affects African Americans and Latinos (Viadero, 2008). As the American economy recovers from the Great Recession and the unemployment rate continues to slowly drop, African Americans are still unemployed at a rate similar to the 2008 jobless rate (Kuhnhenn, 2013). We have already established the historical and cultural impact of race in education, but when poverty is added, the effect is nearly fatal. A 2007 study from the Educational Testing Service, "The Family: America's Smallest School," shows that impoverished white students outscore middle-class African American and Latino students on standardized tests, and poor African American and Latino students score at least two grade levels below poor white students in both mathematics and reading (as cited in Winerip, 2007).

Past Attempts to Close the Achievement Gap

There is no debate anymore about the validity of the achievement gap. Those directly and indirectly affected agree that it exists. Politicians have used it as a rallying point to sell their platform. Universities and scholars have dedicated resources to study and analyze it. Philanthropists have made it a central theme of their charity. Corporations have gotten involved in creating a market-driven system with competition and choice. There has been no shortage of suitors in the pursuit to close the achievement gap.

In the United States, the notion of closing achievement gaps has become synonymous with education reform. From January to June 2011, *Education Week* ran sixty-three stories mentioning achievement gaps (Hess, 2011). In addition, organizations like the Education Trust (www.edtrust.org), the National Education Foundation (www.neafoundation.org), Achievement Gap Educational Foundation, and Uncommon Schools (www.uncommonschools.org) seek to eliminate the gaps in opportunity and achievement across the United States.

The U.S. government has a long history of trying to legislate educational equality. The U.S. Supreme Court ordered school desegregation with its landmark *Brown v. Board of Education of Topeka, Kansas,* decision in 1954. This important court decision rejected the idea of "separate but equal" accommodations, implying that the government cannot legally discriminate against its own citizens (Brown v. Board of Educ., 1954). The federal government tried to close the school-funding gap with the Elementary and Secondary Education Act (ESEA) of 1965 by providing federal funding for schools in at-risk communities. The Education for All Handicapped Children Act of 1975 and the Individuals With Disabilities Education Act (IDEA) of 1990 sought to improve the educational opportunities and quality of education for students with disabilities. All these acts were successful at providing more access and more equitable funding for Americans of all backgrounds, but they were not successful at closing achievement gaps (Shaw, 2008).

No policy embodies the idea of egalitarianism more than the 2002 reauthorization of the ESEA known as No Child Left Behind (NCLB, 2002). NCLB, the signature education policy of President George W. Bush, mandated that all public school students take state-standardized academic assessments annually in both mathematics and reading. The law demanded that each school prepare 100 percent of its student population—without concessions for students based on factors like race, social class, disability, gender, or native language—to pass a state-administered mathematics and reading test by 2014. In the interim, every year leading up to 2014, schools had to meet adequate yearly progress (AYP), a minimum proficiency score on the tests that increased annually. Schools that did not make AYP were hit with sanctions and given unflattering labels.

NCLB ushered in an era of federally driven educational accountability focused on narrowing the chasms between the test scores and graduation rates of students of different incomes and races. As Frederick Hess (2011), director of education policies at the American

Enterprise Institute, notes, "The result was a whole new way of speaking and thinking about the issue. 'Achievement gaps' became school reformers' catchphrase, and closing those gaps became *the* goal of American education policy." Politically, both major parties, Democrats and Republicans, take similar stances on the issue of the achievement gap—both presidents George W. Bush *and* Barack Obama have identified educational equality as a major civil rights issue (Hess, 2011).

NCLB was immediately unpopular with the educational community (Feller, 2006). It seemed acceptable to claim in the school mission statement that the primary purpose of the organization was egalitarian in nature, but it was totally different when it came to practical implementation. The data show that only 1 percent of American schools identified as failing in 2002, according to NCLB criteria, were on track with AYP by 2011 (Carpenter, 2011). NCLB did not accomplish its stated goals and in many ways reinforced inequality. Even when the government mandated that all students achieve, the gaps still existed. We have learned from a history of failed educational policies that the government cannot mandate equality through law. Many initiatives that have come out of these legislative attempts have further contributed to the problem.

Conclusion

Though many would like to believe that we live in an equitable society, history and facts do not support this belief for all members of society. Racism and classism exist, and these realities affect real lives every day. The achievement gap does not exist because of some inherent biological or genetic flaw found in African American and Latino students or insurmountable environmental barriers students of poverty face. It exists, in large part, because a society with a philosophical commitment to equality has not made a practical commitment to equality.

CHAPTER 2

A Practical Commitment to Equality

*Of all our studies, history is best qualified
to reward our research.*

—*Malcolm X*

A strong disconnect exists in U.S. schools between what educators purport to believe and value and the actions they take regarding those values. While schools claim to be committed to equitable treatment and opportunities for all students, the reality reflects a different story. I assert that while many schools talk the talk of egalitarianism, they walk the walk of a meritocratic system. This has created a functional hypocrisy in our schools that perpetuates functional inequality.

Egalitarianism

Merriam-Webster's Collegiate Dictionary (n.d.) defines *egalitarianism* in the following manner.

1: a belief in human equality especially with respect to social, political, and economic affairs

2: a social philosophy advocating the removal of inequalities among people

In a society that lists equality as one of its core values, it would be logical that its systems and institutions embrace egalitarian idealism. This would explain why school mission and vision statements include terms like *all*, *every*, and *each* when referring to its goals for student growth and achievement. However, as chapter 1 demonstrates, the egalitarian ideal that public school systems claim to embrace has not evolved from ideal to reality. Most of the merit has been enjoyed by white and Asian students who speak English well and who come from households where their parents earn middle- or upper-middle-level incomes (Lezotte, 2001).

Stanford University Professors Emeritus David Tyack and Larry Cuban (1995) argue that through these mission and vision statements, U.S. schools have been inundated with the idea that they have to create a utopian environment and embody the idea of equality for the greater society. Consequently, schools have been asked to produce outcomes that are not expected in other vital parts of society like healthcare, economics, and politics. Tyack and Cuban (1995) argue that this expectation creates a positive pressure to improve, but it also creates an unreasonable level of pressure to achieve equality in an environment where inequality appears to be tolerated in many other sectors.

I contend that our best behaviors are driven by goals that seem difficult, and in some cases impossible—like parenting. Parents are entrusted to guide, nurture, and shape the lives of their children and our society's future citizens. It is a tough job, but parents are expected to perform this duty well, with little to no training, and in some cases with limited resources. We don't expect parents to favor one child over the other, and we expect them to instill values in their children that are congruent with those living in our society. Parents don't always succeed, but we expect them to give no less than 100 percent effort and sincerity. I believe that we should have the same expectations for schools.

Meritocracy

The antithesis of *egalitarianism* is a *meritocracy. Merriam-Webster's Collegiate Dictionary* (n.d.) defines a *meritocracy* in the following manner.

> 1: system in which the talented are chosen and moved ahead on the basis of their achievement
>
> 2: leadership selected on the basis of intellectual criteria

This philosophy supports the belief that the talented achieve, and the disinterested and less talented fail. In essence, the cream rises to the top. There are no inalienable rights in a meritocracy; favor has to be earned.

Equality is not the goal of a meritocracy; the goal is to find and reward talent. This philosophy may make perfect sense if we are analyzing the compensation structure of a sales force or picking which player to select in the upcoming professional sports draft, but when we are looking at a guiding philosophy for educating a population of students, it is not quite as appropriate. In my career, I have had the opportunity to teach, coach, and guide thousands of educators, and I have found that the dominant theory of practice is closer to a meritocracy than egalitarianism.

The tension between egalitarianism and a meritocracy plays a major role in the disconnect between the values and actions prevalent in many school systems. *Egalitarianism* sounds good. It has a just ring and tone to it. *Meritocracy* sounds cruel and insensitive, and it would definitely not pass the test of political correctness. I could not imagine that a school would publicly acknowledge its commitment to a meritocracy with a mission statement like:

> Neighborhood Elementary School is committed to separating the gifted from the less able. We will work together to use practices and create systems that allow the talented to soar and condemn those poor souls who are aloof or too immature to take advantage of our offerings.

It would seem logical that a teacher or school administrator would be motivated to differentiate his or her work and resources to tailor services to meet individual student needs and ensure learning for all. Unfortunately, that is not the universal reality. A meritocracy is based on the belief that all members of society or an organization are on a level playing field and that the rules of merit are fair and just. In the 1968 speech "Remaining Awake Through a Great Revolution," Martin Luther King Jr. says, "It's all right to tell a man to lift himself by his own bootstraps, but it is a cruel jest to say to a bootless man that he ought to lift himself by his own bootstraps" (Carson & Holloran, 1998). These words perfectly illustrate how the playing field is not level. As illustrated in the previous chapter, inequity and inequality do exist.

Functional Hypocrisy

Equality is a concept we love in theory but not always in practical application. Equality implies that no person or group is superior or inferior. The concept resonates in the American spirit, and it is a staple in the core belief systems of a democratic society. In fact, it is the first principle that the Declaration of Independence identifies. The second paragraph of this important, foundational document reads: "We hold these truths to be self-evident, that all men are created equal, that they are endowed by their Creator with certain unalienable Rights that among these are Life, Liberty and the pursuit of Happiness."

This seminal document asserts that equality is the foundation for forming a just government and society and that its laws and institutions should be built around this concept. So, it is not surprising that the public school system, an important governmental institution, should be aligned with this concept of equality in theory. To test my theory, I conducted a series of random Internet searches of U.S. school district mission and vision statements. I chose forty random schools of various sizes, demographics, grade configurations, and incomes from every region of the United States, and *every* one of their mission statements was egalitarian.

It is, however, clear that the rhetoric from many schools does not match the facts or their current reality. In fact, there is a *functional hypocrisy* that exists relative to the concept of equality that serves both the beneficiary's and victim's needs. This is at the core of the achievement gap trap, and is connected to the small-talk trap identified by Pfeffer and Sutton (2000). The hypocritical need of school systems and our society to portray egalitarianism, while behaving like a meritocracy, creates an environment of comfort and stagnation. Until there is a thorough examination of the nature of this hypocrisy, equality will never be a reality in schools; it will only be a buzzword used to tickle the ears.

A clear example of this functional hypocrisy is in the 2014 New York State student test scores, particularly in New York City. Ninety New York City schools with black and Latino populations totaling 1,678 students failed to prepare even one of them to meet New York State's learning targets (Brown & Chapman, 2014). In response to these dismal statistics, Devora Kaye, the education department spokesperson, stated, "We are committed to ensuring that all students, regardless of ethnicity or background, receive a high-quality education" (Brown & Chapman, 2014). This story did not receive national headlines. Most would consider the facts associated with this story as sad but not a call to action. I wonder whether the response would be the same if ninety schools failed to pass a single white or upper-middle-class student.

As a young child growing up in the industrial town of Flint, Michigan, in the 1970s and 1980s, I remember this subtle hypocrisy well. I attended elementary and middle school in the Flint Community Schools, or what we called the *city schools*. The city schools were very segregated. Not by law, but by situation. There were several suburban school districts that we all grew to understand were for white people and existed to serve their interests, and the city schools were the best place for black people.

The city schools were powerhouses for sports, and Flint produced some of the most prestigious athletes in the country at that time, like NFL great Andre Rison and NBA legend Glen Rice. The Charles Stewart Mott Foundation provided us with a wide variety of recreational activities, and the school buildings were always vibrant and active with nonacademic activities. It was fun, and I cannot remember anyone complaining. In fact, we loved it! However, academics were a sideshow. There was some subtle emphasis on academic achievement, but the message was clear: school is a place to occupy time until a student either drops out and works in the auto factory or graduates and works in the auto factory. If you are one of the lucky ones, you can become a professional athlete. No one ever articulated these messages overtly, but the focus on leisure and the lack of emphasis on academic achievement and rigor made it unnecessary for the educators to verbalize.

The suburban schools, on the other hand, were the polar opposite. A very clear line was drawn. Suburban schools were places where white and economically affluent minority students attended school to excel academically. Their schools were equipped for academic achievement, their classes were difficult, and it was the haven for smart kids. In fact, whenever a peer from our neighborhood moved to one of the suburban schools, he or she would return to tell us how difficult the classes were and how "boring" the school was. When city schools competed with suburban schools in athletics, the city schools would typically annihilate the suburban schools. When there was a debate or robotics competition, the suburban schools would typically annihilate the city schools. It was our reality. It was comfortable, and both sides seemed to benefit from this separate and unequal reality.

My reality changed significantly in high school. My mother and stepfather informed me that we were moving to the suburbs and that I had to attend a suburban school. It was one of the most difficult moments of my youth. I wondered how I would fit in and whether I was equipped for the academic rigor that I anticipated. I wondered if I would have to give up my cultural identity and assimilate to be accepted and make friends. I approached my parents and asked about the rationale for their decision, and my stepfather gave me an answer that I will never forget. It has shaped me as a person and an educator. He looked at me and said that they wanted my siblings and me to attend *better* schools and have opportunities that he did not enjoy as a child. Up to that point in my life, I never thought that people considered the suburban school to be better. Was there a standard by which to judge schools that I was not aware of at the time? Was society playing a cruel joke on us?

I would discover much later that schools do make a difference, that some prepare students well for their future and some do not, and that our society accepts this reality, though we claim that equality is important. In the 21st century, it is not as simple as suburban versus urban schools. In fact, the majority of American ethnic minority students attend schools in suburban areas (Frankenberg & Orfield, 2012). The hypocrisy is much more complex today. The lines have been redrawn, but the dilemma is still the same: there is a system that does not serve all equally and a society where that reality is palatable.

Dan Lortie (1975), professor emeritus of education at the University of Chicago, explains that educators are the professional victims of their own experience as students. Educators have been socialized in the system in which they practice since they were impressionable four- or five-year-old children. They interact with the organization's norms, values, and methods for at least thirteen years as K–12 students, and in turn, they tend to embrace those values and perpetuate and protect them as professionals. Lortie (1975) calls this phenomenon the *apprenticeship of observation*. He also points out that most educators were successful students in the traditional system, which makes it difficult for them to rationalize substantive change, operating from the mentality of "if it worked for me, it should work for them." We tend to subconsciously repeat what we have experienced, even if it is in conflict with the organization's stated objectives.

Functional Inequality

In 1945, sociologists Kingsley Davis and Wilbert Moore introduced the theory of *functional inequality*. Davis and Moore (1945) argue that inequality is a natural by-product of a progressive society. Talent is not equally distributed, so a progressive society has to decide how it prepares the most talented to inherit important positions and less talented people to hold less important positions in society. Davis and Moore's (1945) argument is based on *functionalism*, which is a premise that social order functions as a result of societal influences and collective goals (Marshall, 1998). I lived that reality as a child. The city schools prepared people for less-impactful positions (in a factory or on the athletic field), and the suburban schools prepared people for the more-impactful positions (professional or decision-making positions).

Similarly, by looking at the statistics in *The Bell Curve* (Herrnstein & Murray, 1994), one could assume equality is a fantasy of the disillusioned, that some people are just smarter and more capable than others, and that instead of rejecting this fact, society should embrace this functional inequality and use its resources to support the genetically and intellectually superior, whom the authors refer to as the *cognitively elite*. This in turn would make life better for the less gifted, or *cognitively dull*. These authors took the debate one step further than Davis and Moore (1945)—they claim that this stratification of cognitive gifts and talents had a racial component attached. The *cognitive elite* are primarily made up of whites and Asians, with a few outliers from other races, and the *cognitively dull* are primarily made up of black and Latino people, with a few outliers from the white and Asian community. This was a quasi-scientific explanation for the difference between the city and suburban schools of my childhood.

After both of these resources were published, there was an immediate outcry of foul play from the research community and the greater society. In a society that claims to value liberty, justice, and equality, these assertions just don't resonate in the psyche. These arguments caused severe cognitive dissonance, and there were hundreds of counterstudies released to refute and marginalize these theories. Stephen Jay Gould (1994), for instance, finds that the statistical models that were used to make their arguments were flawed and that there were too many extraneous variables for the data to be correct. Howard Gardner (1995) argues that more recent cognitive and neuroscience findings were much more reliable when predicting intelligence than race.

The theories developed by this work, and the authors who created it, were attacked not because the greater society truly embraced equality as a functional principle, but because they made the reality of inequality seem barbaric and cold. The authors spoke what many felt and believed but refused to say because verbalizing and affirming functional inequality would upset the functional hypocrisy.

Functional Hypocrisy and Inequality in Closing the Achievement Gap

There have been billions of dollars poured into closing the achievement gap, but the longitudinal data have taught us that the disparity is still present and glaring. As noted previously, it would be logical to expect that a government founded on the principle of equality would be very proactive and genuinely concerned about a trend of inequality, and yet, the functional hypocrisy exists. It is ironic that many efforts to close the achievement gap—such as standardized test scores, adequate yearly progress, and accountability ratings— have actually been exercises in contradiction that support and perpetuate this functional inequality.

Standardized Test Scores

There has been an ageless debate about how to objectively measure student progress. Some scholars argue that standardized tests, though not perfect, provide us with the best opportunity to truly understand the skill level of students and that those who oppose them are only afraid that they will be exposed for underserving students (Thernstrom & Thernstrom, 2003). Others argue that the tests are culturally and economically biased, that they are not a good and valid measure of student knowledge, and that they take valuable instructional time away from teachers who spend all their time teaching to the test (Stake, 1991).

Standardized test scores have been at the center of the discussion and study of the achievement gap on both sides of the argument. It is difficult to improve a variable that can't be measured. But the question remains, Are standardized tests and test scores beneficial in the fight to close the achievement gap, or are they a part of the central problem? Could the instrument of measurement and the data that it produces be tools to perpetuate and solidify performance gaps?

Diane Ravitch is one of the most vocal opponents of using standardized tests and test data to assess student knowledge and teacher and school quality. Ironically, Ravitch was an original architect of NCLB, but after rethinking the logic and approach of the law, she has become one of its biggest challengers. In *Reign of Error: The Hoax of the Privatization Movement and the Danger to America's Public Schools*, Ravitch (2013) gives insight into her analysis of the real intent behind the standardized testing movement and NCLB. She argues that federal programs such as NCLB and President Obama's education program Race to the Top set unreasonable targets for American students, punish schools, and result in teachers being fired if their students underperform, unfairly branding those educators as failures. Ravitch warns that the negative publicity that struggling schools face is just a front for an economic agenda perpetuated by businesses poised to cash in on school-turnaround funds, and that investors are beginning to see it as an emerging market. She goes on further to claim that the loss of power and influence many teacher unions experience and the restructuring of many urban school districts are purposeful and not coincidental. Public humiliation of the public school system is being used as a tool to advance the public outcry for the expansion of charter schools and privatization of struggling public schools and meet the economic agenda of powerful people working behind the scenes.

Adequate Yearly Progress

As previously mentioned, AYP became a high-stakes endeavor once NCLB was put into motion. AYP initiatives introduced schools to the world of test score *disaggregation*. In theory, schools were supposed to analyze a set of test scores reflecting academic performance, and that information would provide each school with valuable information about which students were benefiting most from their academic experience and which students or groups needed special assistance. The provision sounded logical for any school trying to promote equality, but the opposite happened in many cases.

As the reins of NCLB began to tighten and some subgroups— African American, Latino, and impoverished students, in particular— were not making gains at nearly the rate the state and federal governments mandated, resentment and political manipulation began to grow. Schools began to find ways to omit or hide the scores of low-performing subgroups to improve the overall test performance and save the school from public embarrassment (Dizon, Feller, & Bass, 2006). Some schools and school districts with relatively small numbers of poor and minority students lobbied their local legislators to redefine or raise enrollment requirements for a group to be declared a subgroup, so that a small number of students would not negatively affect the accountability rating of the majority (Klein, 2010). The most common response was to drop the requirement for proficiency so low that it would be very difficult for students to fail the test, allowing most schools to meet the AYP provision. Most states set proficiency ratings at *less than 50 percent correct*, and in

Michigan, the state board of education set proficiency on the third-, fourth-, and fifth-grade state tests at a whopping 38 percent correct (Peterson & Hess, 2008).

Accountability Ratings

Not only were schools assessed and AYP status measured using standardized test scores, but NCLB also required schools to be rated on a state standardized accountability system. This provision was to provide parents with a clear understanding of school performance so that they could choose the school they felt was best for their child. *Parental choice* became the catchphrase.

When I was a principal in Michigan, our accountability system was called Education YES! (often shortened to *EdYES!*) (Michigan Department of Education, 2014). The EdYES! system provided each school and the public with a report card and rated schools with letter grades. An *A* was considered *excellent*, and an *F* was considered *failing*. One-third of the analysis was a self-assessment that each school was supposed to fill out and rate. District officials encouraged us to score ourselves very high on the self-assessment in order to maximize our EdYES! rating. The entire self-esteem of a school and a community could rest on what letter grade the state gave the school. How can a school truly be reflective and concentrate on the achievement needs and differentials identified in its data while padding its self-assessment in order to help achieve a better accountability rating and prevent an institutional meltdown?

This practice did not die under the phasing out of NCLB since 2011; states to which the U.S. Department of Education provided waivers, allowing them to operate under alternative terms to NCLB, had to sustain rating systems as a condition of being granted a waiver (U.S. Department of Education, 2013). So, rating schools appears to be here to stay, though the format may change periodically. It seems that it would be more logical to work with struggling schools privately instead of comparing them to other schools in a system of ranking and sorting. This practice has not helped schools become more reflective; it has launched them into survival mode.

Conclusion

Our society publicly states that we want equal academic outcomes in public schooling, but our past and current behaviors have not always supported this declaration. The rhetoric continues, but the inequality still exists, and will continue to exist until a major shift in thinking and behavior occurs. I've investigated how we've gotten to this place in the achievement gap and ways to prepare for change. I argue that to most people, the achievement gap is expected, acceptable, and functional. It exists, in large part, because a society with a philosophical commitment to equality has not made a practical commitment to equality. We first have to acknowledge this fact before we can attempt real cultural change. In the next chapter, I'll discuss critical mindsets that create barriers to change and an essential mindset that will allow you to overcome them, outlining a framework to use to begin addressing cultural change in schools.

CHAPTER 3
Mindset and Cultural Change

Children should be educated and instructed
in the principles of freedom.

—PRESIDENT JOHN ADAMS

Our thoughts matter. How we think and what we think will have a tremendous impact on our activity as human beings and the quality of life that we enjoy. No concept embodies these principles more than the concept of *mindset*, which is the established set of attitudes each person has. It is the summary of our beliefs about the world and how it works, and it acts as the guide for our behaviors and decisions. I assert that the biggest issue related to closing the achievement gap is that we have the wrong mindset. If we can change the mindset, perhaps the strategies, structures, policies, and resources allocated for creating equality in schools have a fighting chance to work. This, in turn, will require enacting cultural change. In this chapter, I will outline the mindsets that can either perpetuate or remedy the inequalities illustrated in the previous chapters. I then suggest a framework for cultural change to use as a guide for developing the necessary mindset in schools to achieve equality for all students.

The Anatomy of a Mindset

To change a mindset, and thus a culture, we must first understand the building blocks and catalysts of the various mindsets at work. Stephen Covey (1989), acclaimed thought leader, identifies two very distinct states of mind that can either promote substantive change or perpetuate stagnation. He calls these two states of mind the *circle of influence* and the *circle of concern*. The circle of influence represents the parts of a person's life or condition that are directly within his or her ability to control. These are things like self-discipline, personal habits, and personal use of time. The circle of concern represents all of the things in the world that are troubling but are not within a person's ability to directly control. These things include issues like world peace and political corruption and even things as simple as people's attitudes. Covey (1989) theorizes that an intense focus on the circle of influence (things that you can directly control) is much more effective than focusing on things that are generally unfair and are beyond a person's direct ability to control. If the achievement gap is going to be closed, students, families, teachers, schools, and communities lagging behind others in academic skill development have to work within their circle of influence first. Improvement begins with looking in the mirror!

Similarly, Glenn Singleton and Curtis Linton (2006), who have been authorities on the construct of race and how it affects educators and educational systems, identify three critical attitudes that all stakeholders must adopt if we truly want to close the achievement gap. The first factor is *passion*. Passion is the level of connectedness educators bring to the antiracism and antipoverty work. One's passion must be strong enough to overwhelm institutional inertia, resistance against change, and the system's resilience or its desire to maintain status quo. The second factor is *practice*. Practice refers to the essential individual and institutional actions taken to effectively educate every student to his or her full potential. The third and final factor is *persistence*. Persistence involves time and energy. Rarely do we dedicate sufficient time to address the achievement gap. Persistence at the institutional level is the willingness of a school system to invest time and energy over the long haul to fix inequality despite slow results, political pressure, new ideas, and systematic inertia. As stated in the introduction, priorities like the Common Core State Standards and new teacher evaluation systems have taken over the organizational attention in school, and there appears to be a dwindling enthusiasm and commitment to achieving academic equity.

Building off of previous research, I have come to identify three distinct mindsets that either contribute to or work to close the racial, ethnic, and socioeconomic achievement gaps.

1. **The superiority mindset:** Those who have convinced themselves that they are superior to others hold this mindset, which guides them to maintain such a perception.

2. **The victim mindset:** Those who enjoy the comforts of not being expected to do very much, and who enjoy the convenience of holding other people responsible for their current station in life hold this mindset.

3. **The liberation mindset:** Those who feel that their beliefs and actions can shape and change reality hold this mindset.

The leading authority on the research of mindset is Carol Dweck. She has written about this topic for decades, and in 2006, she published her most definitive work on the subject, titled *Mindset: The New Psychology of Success*. Dweck's findings shed new light on how we view ourselves and how that view affects our personality. A *fixed mindset* assumes that our character, intelligence, and creative ability are static and unchangeable, and that success is the affirmation of natural or fixed characteristics. In a fixed mindset, people strive to validate their fixed perceptions about themselves at all costs. A *growth mindset* is the antithesis of the *fixed mindset*. People who operate from this mindset thrive on challenge, and they see failure as a natural part of the growth process that helps us to expand and improve upon our existing abilities. These two mindsets, which Dweck claims we develop at a very early age, largely influence our behavior and our approaches to success and failure, eventually influencing our capacity for happiness (Popova, n.d).

The superiority mindset and the victim mindset are two variations of the *fixed mindset* (see chapter 4 for detailed information on the superiority mindset and chapter 5 for more information on the victim mindset). The liberation mindset is a variation within the *growth mindset* as it relates to our collective mentality and behavior around the achievement gap. People with this mindset think through a lens of efficacy. They believe that they are growing and evolving beings and so is society at large. The *liberation mindset* is the key to unlock the potential of those who have suffered and fallen behind in our school systems (for more on the liberation mindset, see chapter 6).

To illustrate these mindsets in the context of the achievement gap in our education system, take the 2009 collaboration between civil rights leader Al Sharpton and former Speaker of the House of Representatives and known political conservative Newt Gingrich—one of the oddest and most vivid examples of the clash between the victim and superiority mindsets. At the request of the U.S. Secretary of Education Arne Duncan, a national education tour focusing on closing the achievement gap was announced. The tour, Partners in Progress, was initially scheduled to visit three cities, with the potential for more if things went well. The foundation of the tour was to promote the principle of education as a basic right, the belief that it should be immune to partisan politics (Sisk, 2009). However, reports circulated that the tour was cut short because of serious philosophical differences between Sharpton and Gingrich that became uncivil and irreconcilable (Siegel, 2011). Sharpton, who has made a life out of petitioning government for fairness and equity, felt that the government needed to invest more money in programs and infrastructure and focus the responsibility for fixing the gap on governmental investment. Gingrich, who is known as a fiscal and social conservative, felt that less government spending and more personal responsibility on the part of underprivileged communities were the way to progress. From his viewpoint, poor and minority communities simply needed a pep talk to pick themselves up by their bootstraps and just work harder. This union was short-lived and illustrates how the victim and superiority mindsets tend to push people further away rather than closer together. These two men, both revered in their respective circles, could not veer away from their closely held views to compromise and create a common solution. Their fight is a microcosm of a greater philosophical disagreement that takes place inside and outside of schools.

The Development of a Theoretical Framework

School culture is a microcosm of society at large; the norms, expectations, behaviors, and, yes, mindsets of education professionals are a manifestation of the greater society. In order to adequately understand and effect such a phenomenon, the development of a theoretical framework is necessary. Historian E. P. Thompson writes:

> Reality is too complex to fully capture in abstractions. Every study selects particular aspects of the world to emphasize, necessarily leaving the rest in a shadowy background. In other words, we must choose what is generally called theoretical frameworks to guide our analysis. (as cited in Thompson, 2001, p. 461)

Frameworks help us understand how abstract ideas interact with one another and make things that are difficult to describe more rational and more easily analyzed. In the attempt to understand and intentionally develop schools into healthy learning environments, I developed the social and political Transforming School Culture (TSC) framework that I describe in the book *Transforming School Culture: How to Overcome Staff Division* (Muhammad, 2009). I want to examine my work on school culture from a broader perspective in this section to help us better understand how we can create egalitarian systems.

Mindset and the Transforming School Culture Framework

The TSC framework (Muhammad, 2009) arranges the participants in a typical school culture into four primary categories: (1) Believers, (2) Tweeners, (3) Survivors, and (4) Fundamentalists. These educators have differing objectives and mindsets that affect their behavior in unique ways.

1. **Believers** are educators who are predisposed to the ideas and programs that support the egalitarian idealism of education. They are willing, and in fact seek, the best professional models to support universal student achievement. Believers are the embodiment of the *liberation mindset.*

2. **Tweeners** are educators who are new to the school culture. These educators are given a cultural probationary period of two to five years to adopt a mindset in the school tug-of-war. This group is critical to school improvement because if high-risk schools do not retain qualified staff members, school reform becomes nearly impossible because long-term initiatives are impossible to sustain. These educators' mindsets are still forming, and the environment's health or toxicity will play a major role in the professional paradigm that they choose as the foundation of their practice for the rest of their career.

3. **Survivors** are educators with one purpose: survival. This group represents a portion of school professionals who have lost their vigor and simply survive from day to day. Survivors lack the will and the skill to overcome demanding circumstances and fall comfortably into mediocrity. Students flounder academically and socially in this environment, and I have found that these types of educators are more prevalent in schools with high numbers of black and Latino students and students from impoverished families—the students who need the most dedicated and skilled teachers available to close the achievement gap. Survivors are the embodiment of the *victim mindset.*

4. **Fundamentalists** are educators who are comfortable with and are defined by the status quo; they organize and work

against any viable form of change. Their goal is to define professional success based on their strengths and capabilities, thus positioning themselves to be "successful." They have many tools that they use to thwart reform initiatives, and without the proper leadership, they are generally successful in doing so. They believe that their way is the only way, and they use systems and influence to protect their personal beliefs and preferences, even when it adversely affects some of the students they serve. Fundamentalists are the embodiment of the *superiority mindset.*

When not properly cultivated, these diverse agendas can lead to staff division and school dysfunction. The interaction of these complex groups of individuals makes school reform difficult at best, and only disciplined and informed leadership is qualified to untangle this web and focus the school professionals on the singular goal of total student success.

The research of Terrence Deal and Kent Peterson (1999) is important to consider when addressing interaction among educators from these varied categories. This research defines school culture as a school's set of norms, values, rituals, beliefs, symbols, and ceremonies that produces a school persona. According to Deal and Peterson, there are two types of cultures: *healthy* and *toxic.* A healthy culture is egalitarian, and a toxic culture is a meritocracy. It is important to point out that Deal and Peterson found that beliefs and attitudes were formed *before* the norms, rituals, and symbols; the collective philosophy of a school develops before the tangible policies, practices, and procedures. So, if we want to see the behaviors of a school change, we must first address the mindset that is the catalyst to the behavior we want to see change. Developing a healthy culture is the key to using the research and strategies specifically designed to close the achievement gap. Because Believers and Fundamentalists both jockey for control of the collective norms and expectations, I want to focus my discussion on their mindsets in particular, which reflect a greater societal battle between egalitarianism and meritocracy.

Team Players

An analysis of the behavior of Believers (liberation mindset) and Fundamentalists (superiority mindset) reveals real differences in philosophy and objective, and these differences drive their behavior. Jim Collins (2001), in his book *Good to Great*, identifies why great companies and organizations consistently outperform average or low-performing companies and organizations. He describes that great organizations have the following three attributes.

1. Disciplined people
2. Disciplined thought
3. Disciplined action

When dealing with the issue of disciplined people, Collins (2001) writes:

> We expected that good-to-great leaders would begin by setting a new vision and strategy. We found instead that they first got the right people on the bus, the wrong people off the bus, and right people in the right seats— and then they figured out where to drive it. The old adage "People are your most important asset" turns out to be wrong. People are not your most important asset; the right people are. (p. 12)

Collins (2001) concurs with Deal and Peterson (1999): aligning everyone's commitments, foci, attitudes, and behaviors with the organizational objectives or progress is nearly impossible. I do not subscribe to the notion that people are innately or inherently right or wrong, but I do believe that there is a difference between productive and unproductive organizational behavior, and thus is the case between the Believers and Fundamentalists.

Believers accept the fact that their role is to help the organization achieve its objective of success for every student. Their focus on this objective guides their behavior, so feedback that illustrates when their work is counterproductive to their goal does not spark a defensive response. They are willing to become reflective and strategic instead of becoming flabbergasted and defensive. Simply stated, the organizational goal supersedes their individual likes and dislikes. They are ready to lend their gifts and talents to confront obstacles and achieve collective success. A Believer is a true team player; a *we*-first as opposed to a *me*-first professional. If every educator behaved this way, all of the great research-based structures and techniques would be implemented with fidelity, and we would see the achievement results that we claim to crave as a society.

Fundamentalists have come to believe that their personal agendas are more important than the collective agenda. Protecting their personal and political interests becomes more important than the needs of the students they are entrusted to serve. They play political games and lobby other members of the organization to buttress their power base, and any change or proposed behavior that is in conflict with their personal needs or desires becomes the object of their destruction. A Fundamentalist is a *me*-first and *we*-second employee. His or her behavior would be what Collins (2001) describes as the behavior of the *wrong people on the bus*. However, I do not advocate targeting people personally—I believe it is more effective to attack the behavior and transform it to be better and more productive by improving communication, building trust, providing training and resources, and building reasonable systems of accountability (Muhammad & Hollie, 2012). John Wooden, the late and legendary University of California, Los Angeles (UCLA), basketball coach who coached more U.S. college basketball teams to national championships than any other coach in history, was asked what it takes to be a good team player. His response was to "consider the rights of others before your own feelings, and the feelings of others before your own rights" (Orr, 2009). Schools are teams of educators with the goal of educating every student, and selfishness and personal agendas are harmful to accomplishing that collective goal of educating every student. Unfortunately, many schools have allowed adults who consider their personal agenda more important than the collective agenda to hijack the focus, energy, and commitment to the most innocent members of our society: our children. Fundamentalism and healthy cultures cannot coexist.

Technical Versus Cultural Change

The TSC framework (Muhammad, 2009) identifies two forms of change at the root of organizational development. These two forms of change are *technical* and *cultural* change. Technical change represents the organization's nonhuman aspects. In a school, technical change can represent things like curriculum, structure, formal policies, and technology. Technical change is a vital component of school development. The second form of change is cultural change. Cultural change would require a change in beliefs, assumptions, and attitudes. In my experience working with schools on change and improvement, cultural change has always been the most challenging of the two forms of essential change.

To simplify the concepts, I created an analogy to make the connection very clear and apparent. A gardener who is serious about developing a bountiful harvest has to be concerned about two very key components of gardening: the *soil* and the *seed*. In organizational development, culture is like soil, and technical change is like a seed. I observed that we have made a heavy investment in strategy and structure (seed) but almost no investment in the human environment or culture (soil). If the great strategies from the top educational researchers can have a fighting chance to work, we have to create a culture that is nurturing enough to implement the strategy or system. I developed the TSC framework to provide a clearer and more rational view of the culture (soil) so that anyone who desired to develop it would understand it better and be able to positively manipulate it. The change in culture begins with a change in mindset, and like all change, the two are linked. As William Glasser (1998) points out, all behavior is based on a personal theory. If we can address the theory, we have a chance to change the behavior.

Conclusion

If schools are to move closer to the egalitarianism idealism, we must first accept that it does not currently exist. Rhetoric and tricky politics have only made the situation worse, and we must lean on a much more progressive and effective set of strategies and paradigms if we hope to truly achieve equality. We need a major shift in mindset; we need a new and healthy school culture. Honest analysis of our thoughts, habits, and beliefs and the institutions that they produce is paramount if we ever hope to truly achieve universal academic success. We cannot solve the problem until we look at it differently. To gain a more thorough understanding of these mindsets, the next three chapters discuss each one in greater depth.

CHAPTER 4

The Superiority Mindset

We were never given the right by our creator
to feel superior to other people.

—Iyanla Vanzant

It is difficult to achieve equality in a society when there is a segment of powerful individuals who have defined themselves as superior and have committed their influence and resources to maintaining that superiority. It is equally as challenging when other people believe that the dominant group represents the standard of excellence and they judge all of their personal behavior and systems by that standard. Common ground is difficult to find unless all parties involved are truly working toward the same end. I contend that the time, scholarship, effort, and resources put forth to address the achievement gap were doomed to fail from their inception because there are people with a superiority mindset who have a vested interest in being defined as superior to others, and they will seek to protect it. This hardened set of belief systems creates the foundation for fundamentalist behavior in schools.

Theories About the Superiority Mindset

One of the oldest theories concerning people's need or desire to feel superior is 17th century British philosopher Thomas Hobbes's superiority theory. According to Hobbes, humor is a natural extension of a person's need to feel superior to others (Lloyd & Sreedhar, 2014). The need to laugh at the folly and shortcomings of others is a root cause of humor and becomes a psychological coping mechanism that allows a person to feel superior to others while ignoring his or her own personal flaws. The key components of this theory are *paternalism* and *patronization*. In Hobbes's view, people have a need to exist above the standard of mediocrity, and humor and satire exist to remind people that lesser planes of existence are real, but ultimately, we are superior to that standard. This theory has been studied and challenged many times, but it is respected as a seminal work that launched the academic study of this human personality trait.

One of the most definitive works in understanding why people would have a need to feel superior to others comes from a contemporary of Sigmund Freud named Alfred Adler. According to Adler's theory, each of us is born into the world with a sense of inferiority. We start as a weak and helpless child and strive to overcome these deficiencies by becoming superior to those around us. He called this struggle *striving for superiority*, and he saw this as the driving force behind all human thoughts, emotions, and behaviors (Heffner, 2002).

Adler believed that feelings of inferiority drive people who strive to be accomplished writers, powerful businesspeople, or influential politicians. These excessive feelings of inferiority can also have the opposite effect. As this need for superiority grows and success becomes overwhelmingly absent, we can develop an *inferiority complex* (see chapter 5, page 79). This belief leaves us feeling incredibly less important and deserving than others—helpless, hopeless, and unmotivated to strive for the superiority that would make us complete. If Adler's theory holds true, then a person who equated superiority with success would have to give up his or her feeling of accomplishment to live in an equal society. Success and superiority cannot be made synonymous if we truly value equality (Heffner, 2002).

Another compelling idea related to the superiority mindset is Jim Sidanius and Felicia Pratto's (1999) research on *social dominance orientation* (SDO). SDO is a psychological trait that predicts a person's level of *preference* for social hierarchy. SDO scales have been developed to assess how people lean on issues of egalitarianism and social dominance, and they include a series of statements that subjects are asked to respond to on a scale from one to seven to indicate their level of agreement or disagreement. The items on the SDO assessment are as follows.

1. Some groups of people are simply inferior to other groups.

2. In getting what you want, it is sometimes necessary to use force against other groups.

3. It's OK if some groups have more of a chance in life than others.

4. To get ahead in life, it is sometimes necessary to step on other groups.

5. If certain groups stayed in their place, we would have fewer problems.

6. It's probably a good thing that certain groups are at the top and other groups are at the bottom.

7. Inferior groups should stay in their place.

8. Sometimes other groups must be kept in their place.

9. It would be good if groups could be equal.

10. Group equality should be our ideal.

11. All groups should be given an equal chance in life.

12. We should do what we can to equalize conditions for different groups.

13. Increased social equality is beneficial to society.

14. We would have fewer problems if we treated people more equally.

15. We should strive to make incomes as equal as possible.

16. No group should dominate in society. (Sidanius & Pratto, 1999, p. 67)

The SDO scale assesses individual orientation, but it has also been studied as a social construct, as it can be applied to structures including corporate environments, government, law enforcement, and schools. SDO is based in evolutionary psychology theories that suggest humans are predisposed to express social dominance under certain conditions. The theory also takes into account temperament and personality (Fischer, Hanke, & Sibley, 2012). This explains why societies that have high levels of diversity tend to create a hierarchical structure that benefits some groups at the expense of other groups. Schools are no exception to this principle.

Components of the Superiority Mindset

The superiority mindset is thus rooted in three traits that reflect the various superiority theories and scales.

1. **Paternalism:** The need to be in control of others (Hobbes's view)

2. **Competition:** The demand to be better than others in ability (Adler's view)

3. **Authority:** The desire to set the standard of acceptable behavior and define oneself and others through that lens (SDO's principles)

As it relates to dominance and superiority in the United States, the prevailing mentality is that white skin and European origin coupled with middle- or upper-class income equal superiority. This superiority mindset dominates the social, political, and educational landscape in the United States and guides greater society's policies, practices, and behaviors, and it has a profound impact on achieving equity in American schools. I want to be clear and state for the record that there is nothing wrong possessing white skin or European heritage and achieving middle- or upper-income levels. In fact, I would expect members of those communities to be proud of their accomplishments and heritage and celebrate them. However, it becomes problematic when members of any community view their heritage, culture, or norms as the standard that all should subscribe to and use their influence to dominate people who may be of a different background or income level, especially when they publically claim that equality is important.

Paternalism

When a group has achieved dominance over others, paternalism is one of the ways that it protects its dominance. Paternalism is a policy or practice from people in positions of authority that restricts freedom and responsibilities in the supposed best interest of their subordinates. In essence, paternalism is the need to give the *appearance* that one is helping someone less fortunate as a tool to maintain dominance. It humanizes the process of dehumanization.

We can never have a real substantive debate about equality as long as a superior-inferior relationship exists between human beings. I contend that most of the debate about the achievement gap and equality in general has been addressed from a paternalistic standpoint, and it remains a barrier to achieving true equality. A paternalistic attitude will not allow an individual, institution, or society to commit to Singleton and Linton's (2006) three critical attitudes for change introduced in chapter 3 (page 52).

The problem of the achievement gap is both social and systemic, and paternalistic attempts to shine light on the subject with no real desire to fix and overhaul the problem are hypocritical. Tomas Arciniega (1977) describes this dilemma:

> Public education has successfully shifted the blame for failure of schools to meet the needs of minority students on the shoulders of the clients that they serve. They have pulled off the perfect crime, for they can never be held accountable, since the reason for failure in school is said to be the fault of poor homes, cultural handicaps, linguistic deficiencies, and deprived neighborhoods. The fact that schools are geared primarily to serve monolingual, white, middle-class and Anglo clients is never questioned. (p. 52)

The problem of equity in schools cannot be viewed as a black, white, Latino, or poor problem. It has to be looked at as a human problem. Anything less than this paradigm will lead to paternalism and lip service that does not lead to change. It will perpetuate the problem under the guise of interest in solving the problem.

I saw paternalism in action in 2000 when I was an assistant principal and was asked to attend a diversity conference and represent my school. The conference was very well organized, and the program included cultural expressions from Africa, Asia, North America, and Central and South America. These cultural expressions were demonstrated through dance, literature, music, and food. After settling into the conference for a few hours, a few things became very apparent.

First, most people in attendance were ethnic minorities dominated by a heavy African American, Latino, and Native American presence. I thought to myself, "Where are all of the white people?" If there was a true desire to create mass awareness of the value of non-European cultures, shouldn't there have been a larger presence of white educators and community members? Secondly, all of the cultural representations were in nonpolitical and noneconomic areas of expression. I saw this as an expression of tokenism. There was recognition but not recognition in the areas that make up the core of an advanced society. Finally, I became painfully aware that there was no real agenda associated with this conference. There was no substantive discussion or presentation about how to achieve equity in school funding, curriculum, assessment, policies, or any other area that would challenge the status quo. It was innocuous entertainment meant to placate. The sponsors could say that they spent time and resources to shine light on cultures and traditions of people of non-European heritage without upsetting the already established system of power. It was paternalism in action.

Competition

The superiority mindset requires that people view human development through the lens of competition. In essence, personal and group value are determined relative to the status of other individuals and groups. The individual or group who performs better on a given scale is better than others who underperformed. This belief has clouded the judgment of people engaged in the process of achieving equity both inside and outside school.

During my many years as a practitioner and consultant, I have often heard people talk about moving into the *best neighborhoods* and enrolling their children in the *best schools*. No one has ever explained to me exactly what those terms mean, but a 2009 study (Wells & Roda, 2009) on parent perceptions of school quality and school choice reveals some issues in the fight for educational equality. The study finds that there are clear definitions of *good school* and a *bad school* to white and black parents. The study concludes both white and black parents tend to view school quality through the same two lenses: high white student enrollment and high economically privileged student enrollment. In summary, white and black parents' perceptions of a school's quality increase as the percentage of white and economically affluent students increases (Wells & Roda, 2009).

The book *Choosing Homes, Choosing Schools* (Lareau & Goyette, 2014) sheds new light on the real factors that determine home and school choices in modern America. The authors identify home and school choice as two of the most important life decisions that an American citizen and family can make. They describe making the right choice synonymous with acquiring an *asset*. The most coveted asset is known as the *gold standard*, and it is described as moving into a racially exclusive area of predominantly white and Asian residents who have achieved an upper-middle-class income. Thus, living in a racially and economically exclusive neighborhood is a sign that a person has distinguished him- or herself from the pack and can justify earning an advanced degree or saving a large down payment for a home in an exclusive neighborhood. According to Lareau and Goyette (2014), it is viewed as one of life's most prized assets.

A prime example of the competitiveness within the superiority mindset is the debate over implementing the Common Core State Standards, which became a national, hot-button issue in 2013. At the heart of the debate are assessment systems that report student progress on mastery of the standards. The assessments test student knowledge at a much deeper level and require higher levels of rigor and proficiency.

Secretary of Education Arne Duncan, who has been a longtime supporter of the standards because he feels that they elevate the academic expectations of students and the quality of teaching in American schools, has been battling hot opposition from many states that oppose implementation. State governments have been receiving pressure, primarily from their most affluent communities who achieve at the highest levels of the system, for many different reasons. In November 2013, Secretary Duncan addressed a national audience of state superintendents to encourage them not to back away from the new, more rigorous standards. He says he finds it:

> fascinating that some of the opposition to the Common Core State Standards has come from white suburban moms who—all of a sudden—their child isn't as brilliant

as they thought they were, and their school isn't quite as good as they thought they were. (as cited in Strauss, 2013)

The tone of his comment was condescending and sarcastic, but it was a challenge to leaders to look beyond political expediency and make a decision that could possibly be in the best interest of all American students. It should be easy to anticipate that those with a fundamentalist attitude about their gold standard and beliefs about life and achievement through a superiority mindset attacked Mr. Duncan aggressively. In fact, the comments on the online article contain death threats and attacks on his personal credibility. I believe that everyone has the right to his or her own opinion when it comes to public policy debate, but for someone to be moved to make death threats against a public official who challenges established assumptions and norms perfectly illustrates how difficult it is to change a competitive environment that a superiority mindset is influencing. If student learning equity is achieved, and we create an egalitarian system of schooling, we eliminate the exclusivity of the gold standard. Thus, the development of an equitable education system would undermine the theory of Alfred Adler.

Authority

The superiority mindset's final component is the desire to establish authority and set the standard of success for all groups. It is the most subtle of the three components, but it is also the most insulting. Equality is difficult to achieve if one group believes that it has the right to define success and progress for the collective. It would require others of a different cultural or social orientation to acquiesce to the dominant construct or risk being ostracized and devalued. In the United States, the standard of success is defined through a white and middle-class lens. As Terence Burnham and Dominic Johnson (2005) explain, "It is white culture that primarily establishes the standards for all intra-racial and interracial group interactions. This white culture dictates to some degree how, when, and where other racial groups determine, develop, and honor their own cultures" (p. 115). The belief that progress is achieved when black, Latino, and impoverished students behave and achieve like white middle-class students is problematic. It creates an illusion that white middle-class students, and in turn their values, represent the model of success and achievement that all students should strive to emulate.

The paper *White Is a Color!* (Singleton, 1997) introduces the concept of *whiteism*. Whiteism is "(1) not recognizing white as a dominant color nor the unearned power and privileges associated with having white skin and (2) having a sense of white entitlement but lacking awareness of the experiences and perspectives of non-white-skinned people" (Singleton, 1997, p. 1). The article confronts the issue of racial privilege and underscores that white people rarely have to be forced to acknowledge the reality of their skin-color privilege because it has been universally accepted as the *standard*. Glenn Singleton (1997) claims that when confronted with the notion of racial privilege, white people often struggle to see it as real or valid.

The issue of privilege and the definition of success can be very problematic when trying to create a system of equality. The brief *Bridging Cultures in Our Schools* (Trumbul, Rothstein-Fisch, & Greenfield, 2000) asserts that white culture and cultures of color tend to define success very differently. Through an analysis of black and Latino culture, Elise Trumbul et al. (2000) find some stark differences. The authors assert that white culture defines success in the following ways.

1. Fostering independence and individual achievement

2. Promoting self-expression, individual thinking, and personal choice

3. Associated with egalitarian relationships and flexibility in roles (e.g., upward mobility)

4. Understanding the physical world as knowable apart from its meaning for human life

5. Associated with private property, individual ownership (Trumbul et al., 2000, p. 3)

Cultures of color tend to view success in the following ways.

1. Fostering interdependence and group success

2. Promoting adherence to norms and group consensus

3. Associated with stable, hierarchical roles (dependent on gender, family background, age)

4. Understanding the physical world in context of its meaning for human life

5. Associated with shared property, group ownership (Trumbul et al., 2000, p. 3)

These core value differences alone can explain a lot of the struggle that students of color face when making critical decisions about their behavior and effort in school. When school-home values collide, a choice has to be made. The student either assimilates or chooses to reject his or her indigenous values in lieu of achieving success in school based on the white standard. John Ogbu (2003), anthropology professor at the University of California at Berkeley, summarizes this phenomenon with the phrase *acting white*. He characterizes acting white as a choice that students of nonwhite heritage in American schools have to make about assimilating to the dominant white construct in school. This results in achieving the success the institution defines or students adhering to their ethnic culture's social norms and achieving the success their culture defines. This is a choice most white students do not have to make.

Class privilege is also a prevalent factor when trying to develop a construct of equality. The dominant view of intelligence, sophistication, and well-being is viewed through the lens of upper- and middle-class incomes. Oscar Lewis (1998) is a leading scholar in the study of the culture of poverty. He writes:

> People with a culture of poverty have very little sense of history. They are a marginal people who know only their own troubles, their own local conditions, their own neighborhood, and their own way of life. Usually, they do not possess the knowledge, the vision or the ideology to see the similarities between their problems and those of others like themselves elsewhere in the world. In other words, they are not *class conscious*, although they are very sensitive indeed to status distinctions. When the poor become class conscious or members of trade union organizations, or when they adopt an internationalist outlook on the world they are, in my view, no longer part of the culture of poverty although they may still be desperately poor. (p. 7)

In other words, poverty creates a set of destructive and learned behaviors that society can change with the proper advocacy and tools. However, both achieving advocacy and assembling the right toolbox have proven difficult.

Consider Reading First, which is a federally sponsored reading initiative primarily aimed at providing early intensive reading instruction and resources for poor prekindergarten through grade 2 students. In 2008, the U.S. Department of Education declared it a failure (Toppo, 2008). The U.S. Department of Education invested over $1 billion per year during the plan's implementation but found that the initiative did not have any measurable impact on aggregate reading levels. So, while the financial resources for reading improvement were provided, they did not result in accelerated reading comprehension for the United States' most financially disadvantaged students.

Conclusion

The TSC framework addresses a disruptive force in schools manifested in a group called Fundamentalists. Fundamentalists exist outside of school as well. The greatest connection between Fundamentalists inside school and the superiority mindset that exists in our society is *denial*. Fundamentalism is a strong adherence to a set of belief systems, even in the face of criticism or clear evidence that the belief system is flawed or counterproductive to collective goals. The primary goal of our education system is to achieve egalitarianism, though our data say we are closer to a meritocracy. We cannot make a difference in our pursuit for equality in a social or professional environment where rigid belief systems and values go unchallenged in the face of the change necessary to create better learning environments and outcomes for all students. We cannot pursue equality when our value systems favor one group over another, especially when we lack the courage to even discuss the problem objectively.

CHAPTER 5

The Victim Mindset

No one can make you feel inferior
without your consent.

—ELEANOR ROOSEVELT

If equality is to become a reality, the onus cannot lie on the shoulders of one group. Dan Lortie (1975) writes that "it is illogical to expect a group of people who have personally benefited from a system to become the catalyst for changing the system" (p. 74). I do not begrudge communities and school systems that strive for excellence for their students, but I believe that they are responsible for supporting policies and creating an atmosphere that protects their superior ranking to the detriment of other communities, schools, and students. So, what is the responsibility of the oppressed?

In a seminal 1951 work, Eric Hoffer, award-winning moral and social philosopher, sums up the dilemma of the oppressed perfectly:

> Discontent by itself does not invariably create a desire for change. Other factors have to be present before discontent turns into dissatisfaction. One of these is a sense of power. Those who are awed by their surroundings do not think of change, no matter how miserable their condition. When our mode of life is so precarious as to make it patent that we cannot control

the circumstances of our existence, we tend to stick to
the proven and the familiar. (p. 7)

Mass change is the result of a burning desire to realize change
and the belief that one has the power to change not just oneself but
also one's environment. I believe that that desire is missing in the
communities and schools that teach students who are at the low end
of the achievement gap. They share a sense of victimization that does
not allow them to use the tools at their disposal, nor does it provide
them with the courage to challenge and demand change from a
system that has been unfair and oppressive.

Theories About the Victim Mindset

One of the most fascinating psychological studies on the effects
of inferiority is the study of self-pity. *Self-pity* is the psychological
state of an individual in perceived adverse situations who has not
accepted the situation and does not have the confidence nor compe-
tence to cope with it. Such a person believes he or she is the victim
of unfortunate circumstances or events and is therefore deserving of
condolence. Self-pity is a negative emotion that does not generally
help deal with adverse situations. However, in a social context, it
may result in others offering sympathy or advice. In essence, self-pity
is a coping mechanism that allows a person to receive the positive
emotion of condolence without the painful work of transformation
(Stöber, 2003).

Self-pity also relieves a person from a sense of personal responsibility (Klein, 1951). If a person or group concludes that a low station
in life is someone else's doing, then responsibility for that condition
and fixing that condition will lie on others' shoulders. This can create a great sense of psychological relief that encourages a person or
organization to disassociate from fixing the problem. I argue that
self-pity has caused a sense of irresponsibility that has contributed
greatly to the lack of movement in closing the achievement gap.
Until students, schools, and communities who are struggling to

improve achievement realize that even in the face of extreme external conditions, they are primarily responsible for raising their own
level of performance, no strategy or resource from the outside can
be effective.

One of the most definitive works on the issue of victimization is
the research on *learned helplessness*. American psychologist Martin
Seligman (1975) popularized this theory. Learned helplessness occurs
when organisms (such as people or animals) endure uncomfortable
situations after continuously experiencing aversive stimuli, because
they cannot control the situation. This condition can impact a person
at many different levels. It can adversely affect physical and psychological health. People can feel this impact through the overproduction
of hormones like cortisol that adversely affect mood and disposi-
tion (Sullivan et al., 2012). Learned helplessness can even produce
a motivation problem. Individuals who have failed at tasks in the
past conclude erroneously that they are incapable of improving their
performance. This might set students behind in academic subjects
and dampen their social skills. Students with learned helplessness typically fail academic subjects and are less intrinsically motivated than
others. In turn, these students will give up trying to gain respect or
advancement through the academic performance (Stipek, 1988). So,
as it relates to the issue of the achievement gap, learned helplessness
is most damaging in the area of *motivation*—not just for students
but for the entire system as well. In chapter 1, I established that
the achievement gap is one of the most comprehensively studied
academic issues in the history of the public school system. Schools
do not lack access to the knowledge and skills necessary to close the
gap, but many lack the motivation and will necessary to implement
the strategies.

Another important idea in the study of inferiority and victimization is the *inferiority complex*. This is another component of Alfred
Adler's theory of human development that stems from a natural
feeling of inadequacy (as cited in Mosak & Maniacci, 1999). Adler
notes that the feeling of inadequacy motivates a person to achieve

great things or, if it becomes too overwhelming, it makes a person stagnant or even regressive. Through discouragement or failure, those with an inferiority complex lack self-worth, have doubt and uncertainty, and feel they do not measure up to society's standards. It is often subconscious and is thought to drive afflicted individuals to overcompensate, resulting either in spectacular achievement or extreme antisocial behavior (Mosak & Maniacci, 1999).

People most at risk for developing an inferiority complex include people who show signs of low self-esteem or self-worth, are of an ethnic minority, have low socioeconomic status, or have a history of depression symptoms (Mosak & Maniacci, 1999). Students who are constantly criticized or do not live up to parents' expectations may also develop this complex. It can also develop in organizations and communities under similar conditions. People inside and outside schools who serve large black, Latino, and poor populations have perpetuated an assumption that these schools are "bad," and the students and educators within these institutions in many cases believe this, creating a psychological stalemate that makes progress nearly impossible (Mosak & Maniacci, 1999).

Components of the Victim Mindset

After a review of the literature and psychological theories cited previously, I have concluded that the victim mindset contains three major components.

1. **Irresponsibility (self-pity):** Maintaining that others are responsible for one's failures and successes

2. **Low motivation (learned helplessness):** Being pacified by comfort over accepting the fight and discomfort that come with substantive change

3. **Low expectations (inferiority complex):** Avoiding disappointment by accepting an inferior status and the belief that disparities are normal

The combination of these three factors can be fatal to a school and community's fight for academic equality. They create a mindset that is destructive, stagnant, and counterproductive.

Irresponsibility

As a child, one of the first lessons that I learned about being a socially well-adjusted human being was the principle of responsibility. Everyone has a role and certain duties that he or she needs to perform in order to have a productive home, community, nation, and world. Chapter 1 established the fact that racism and classism exist, and they create a high level of stress and anxiety for those who are victims of these realities, but they do not excuse a person from being an active agent in his or her personal pursuit of happiness.

There are certain fundamental building blocks for learning that have to be established at home, and parents and communities have to take responsibility for addressing and fixing these issues. The Home Observation for Measurement of the Environment (HOME) Inventory investigates the norms and values that students are exposed to before kindergarten and the result on academic performance (Jencks & Phillips, 1998). The scale ranks families in terms of both the cognitive stimulation and the emotional support that they provided for their children. Cognitive stimulation is measured by noting, for example, the number of children's books in the home, the frequency with which a parent read to a child, and how much effort was made to teach the alphabet, numbers, and colors. It also takes into account visits to parks, museums, and retail stores. Emotional support is somewhat more subjective, but the scale measures mother-child interactions, expressions of affection, patient attention to a child's questions, and nonphysical discipline.

When the study was published, the scale revealed pronounced racial differences for both black and Latino parents. Black and Latino parents scored nine and ten points below the white average, respectively, on a one-hundred-point scale regarding the extent to which their homes provided cognitive stimulation to young children

(Jencks & Phillips, 1998). In terms of emotional support, the gap was much wider for black homes than Latino, though they both lagged behind the average white home. The black gap was twelve points below the white average, and the Latino gap was four points below the white average. The larger gap for black families was explained by the fact that 67 percent of black children come from homes with a single female head of household, who was typically more stressed and less patient with her children's emotional needs as compared to families with two parents sharing responsibility for their children's emotional needs (Jencks & Phillips, 1998). The scale is not perfect, but the researchers found a correlation to performance of academic tasks in schools.

Improving the rating on this scale is totally within the scope of a parent's influence. Many items are simply a matter of choice. Some readers might interpret my analysis to be paternalistic, but there are certain conditions that stimulate intellect and others that dull intellect. Using resources to buy more books instead of video games, taking a child to a museum as opposed to an amusement park, and turning off the television and having a conversation with a child to build vocabulary and a social bond are things that are within a parent's grasp if we are serious about achieving equality in academic outcomes.

Another area for growth in responsibility is in homework or out-of-school assignments. There has been a lot of controversy about the value or utility of homework, but that is not the focus of this analysis. What we do know is that students who take responsibility for practicing concepts outside of school and make completing those academic tasks a high priority tend to perform better on assessments of academic skills (Wilson, 1987). A 1990 study of American tenth-grade students assessed the correlation between perceived student effort and achievement (Farkas, 1996). One area measured academic practice outside school. The study finds that black students who rated themselves as "working as hard as they could every day" reported spending 3.9 hours on out-of-school study per week compared to 4.2 hours for Latinos, 5.4 hours for whites, and 7.5 hours for Asian students. There is obviously a gap between how these groups perceive working to personal capacity.

On the flip side, we know that students who choose leisure activities like television to fill their idle time actually regress academically (Hattie, 2009). During a five-day school week, the average American student watches twelve hours of television. Impoverished students, regardless of race, watch nearly sixteen hours of television; Latino students watch fifteen hours of television; and black children watch a staggering twenty-five hours of television per school week (U.S. Department of Education, Office for Civil Rights, 2014). These are learned habits that only community members and parents can address. Schools can champion awareness, but the power to change this starts at home. Again, these are habits that can be directly influenced in the home and reinforced at school. These issues have nothing to do with corrupt or discriminatory policy. These are matters of personal choice.

Low Motivation

At the very heart of the improvement process is a personal or collective desire to improve. We refer to this desire as *motivation*. A person or group that lacks motivation is not very likely to improve. One of the key factors that produce the victim mindset is low motivation. Low motivation is a product of learned helplessness, which makes it more palatable to accept a precarious situation than to accept the pain associated with transforming that situation. The obstacles may seem like the five-thousand-pound elephants in the room that seem to be easier to ignore than to organize efforts to eliminate.

If there are unhealthy perceptions or structures present in a school, creating a system of equitable achievement is nearly impossible. Educators, schools, parents, and students must confront these barriers internally to develop the type of collective focus necessary to properly educate every child. Specifically, there are three barriers to high levels of motivation; I refer to these as *predeterminations* (Muhammad, 2009).

1. Perceptual (educators' perceptions)
2. Intrinsic (students' and parents' perceptions)
3. Institutional (institutional policies and barriers)

The first elephant necessary to confront is the presence of negative perceptions about a school's students. These disadvantageous perceptions may be found in educators' long-held stereotypes they brought with them to the school. In schools that struggle with the victim mindset, stereotypes staff hold about black, Latino, and impoverished students undermine motivation. Stereotyping is a natural function of the human mind. It helps us understand a complex world in simple terms, though it also causes us to sometimes oversimplify. Walter Lippmann (1922), one of the earliest scholars of stereotyping, describes it like this:

> There is an economy in this. For the attempt to see all things freshly and in detail, rather than as types and generalizations, is exhausting, and among busy affairs practically out of the question. There is neither time nor opportunity for intimate acquaintance. Instead, we notice a trait which marks a well known type, and fill in the rest of the picture by means of the stereotypes that we carry in our heads. (pp. 88–89)

People are presented with mental models about how the world works on a daily basis. In an attempt to understand the world, everyone develops mental models that can become fixed about certain groups of people. Stereotyping does not make a person inhumane or unethical; however, when these mental models adversely affect student groups, such as black, Latino, and impoverished students, stereotyping produces a clash that educators have to resolve before they can agree about organizational purpose and behavior. If educational professionals cannot come to a philosophical agreement, disagreement will manifest itself in poor practice and low motivation.

Negative stereotypes can overwhelm educators because they are then saddled with the burden of educating students they don't understand and don't value. This is a self-imposed psychological burden.

A comprehensive study of five middle schools involved in school restructuring in Philadelphia, titled *Listening to Urban Kids: School Reform and the Teachers They Want* (Wilson & Corbett, 2001), documents the effect of teachers' expectations and perceptions on student performance. Students identified that teachers who "stayed on them and made them be successful" (p. 64) provided a rich learning environment. The authors, Bruce Wilson and H. Dickson Corbett (2001), also find that teachers who students identify as being invested in their success "involved students in constructivist and experiential learning, and experienced better student conduct, grades, and scores on standardized tests" (p. 42).

Alternatively, Wilson and Corbett (2001) describe teachers who were frozen in their negative images and stereotypes of their students. One teacher notes that she was "scared" of her students because she had never been in an "urban" environment and describes her experience as a "daily battle between teacher and student for classroom control" (p. 34). A student describes his experience like this: "My science teacher is scared of us so we mostly work out of the book. We do vocabulary. We read the chapter and get the vocabulary words. After each section in the book, we do a section review" (p. 43). The stereotypes that the teachers carried about urban students produced a level of fear of violence, verbal combativeness, and apathy that restricted their ability to implement instructional strategies like cooperative learning that were rich and engaging. Instead, they settled for mundane tasks like silent reading and book work to fill time and survive the experience, which do little to develop the students cognitively. Thus, the educator's perception about the student has a profound effect not only on his or her will to teach but also on teaching methods. Despite the district's investment in brain- and research-based instructional strategies, Wilson and Corbett (2001) find that these "teachers opted to rely on instructional strategies that were primarily suited to one style or intelligence rather than to several" (p. 34). As such, the students in the five schools had totally different educational experiences based on the teacher's perceptions. Consequently, schools of teachers with these negative stereotypes about their students have frequent teacher turnover. Leaders who are not willing to deal with these psychological barriers are not ready to develop a school that guarantees equity. This cannot be mandated from legislative chambers, and it is not the responsibility of the privileged. It is a metamorphosis that schools and communities have to initiate and experience for themselves.

Stereotyping is a two-way street. Professional educators represent only a part of the entire school community. A student's self-perception plays a major role in his or her success in school. If educators form broad and rigid assumptions based on persistent images and societal expectations, naturally, students and community members might develop similar stereotypes about themselves based on these stimuli.

Educating and motivating students properly is difficult if a teacher is working with students who have negative perceptions about their place in school and their ability to excel in school. The teaching and learning process requires that students practice curricular concepts outside school and actively engage with instruction during school. As noted previously, it is clear that all students do not enter school predisposed to these characteristics for many different reasons, including their negative perceptions about themselves (Viadero, 2010). Students play a major role in their own educational development, and if they perceive their potential negatively, it will affect their behavior and productivity. In fact, Michael Fullan (2003) identifies *student engagement* as the first critical step in the education process. Students own half of that process.

The development of a collective focus on success means that educators have to be up to the challenge of not only changing some long-held negative stereotypes about students but also helping students overcome long-held negative stereotypes about themselves. So, the adult perceptual transformation must precede the student intrinsic transformation. In fact, research on highly effective schools notes that the adult's desire for student success has to be stronger than the student's will to fail (Green, 2009). This concept, commonly referred to as *efficacy*, is a prerequisite to effectively changing negative student self-image. Former Secretary of Health, Education, and Welfare John Gardner (1988) explains, "Fostering self-efficacy, helping people to believe in themselves, is one of an educator's highest duties" (p. 1). The school system did not create the problem of poor self-concept that the student has, but the school has to accept some of the responsibility to be an agent in fixing the problem if its goal is to achieve high levels of academic achievement.

Finally, a school must be willing to analyze internal barriers to achieving its goals by confronting their *institutional predeterminations*. We must be willing to recognize that no sane organization can move forward with policies, practices, structures, or procedures that make achieving our collective goals more difficult. Educators at every level must sit down and reasonably review standard policies and procedures and align them with organizational goals.

Healthy cultures recognize that there will be obstacles to motivation, which are a product of members' own personal socialization, a student's personal socialization, or long-established organizational barriers. Instead of spending their time complaining about the issues, members must seek to understand the issues and develop policies, practices, and procedures that address the issues. Low motivation is an internal problem that only the students, families, and community at large can resolve.

Low Expectations

Expectations for success start at home. Parents are typically the first important socializing influence in their children's lives, and a substantial body of research indicates that parental expectations have a major impact on their children's values, behavior, and goals (Snyder et al., 2003). Children are also exposed to other areas of socialization and form expectations from peers, siblings, the media, and other sources of popular culture (Cotton, 1989). In a study of family expectations of student academic achievement, 81 percent of white parents thought a C represented a bad grade compared to 52 percent of Latino parents, 44 percent of black parents, and 58 percent of parents with an income below the national poverty line (Akey, 2006).

The home is a powerful agent in creating student academic expectations, but the school is even more influential. The topic of school influence on student academic expectations and performance has been documented as far back as the 1960s. Many students have proven that high student academic expectations at school can overcome low expectations at home (Tauber, 1998). According to Tauber, schools that overcome low expectations at home generally have the following characteristics.

- Create a safe, structured, and comfortable learning environment in each classroom that is culturally responsive
- Regularly display high-quality student work
- Have teachers that think, plan, and make decisions to ensure strategic teaching on a daily basis
- Implement high-level student questioning techniques during instruction
- Provide multiple opportunities for students to display content mastery

All of these techniques are within the scope of a school's influence if it has the will to universally implement them.

In my work with schools, I have found that many schools identified for needing improvement don't expect much from their students and become angry at outsiders who do. Some scholars have referred to this phenomenon as the *soft bigotry of low expectations* (McIntyre, 2008).

During a telephone conversation with a principal in a school district that I had the opportunity to work with on a long-term basis, the soft bigotry of low expectations raced into my consciousness. The principal had informed me that his school made huge gains on the state academic achievement test and his school was no longer on the state school failure list. I congratulated him and his staff because that was a huge sign of progress and a testimony to their work together as a school community. As the conversation progressed, he informed me that one associate superintendent in his district publically congratulated him at a principal's meeting, and she scolded other principals in the district for not achieving the same level of student academic proficiency achieved at his school. He proudly told me that the district administrator publicly said that he was an example of what good leadership looked like, and the other schools had no excuses because "they have twice the number of white students in their schools, and they had no excuse for low test scores." Instead of being offended that the district administrator would publicly associate expectation of student achievement with students' skin color, he was very proud of acknowledgment. The principal's attitude toward the administrator's comment is a product of conditioning.

The government, at all levels, in its attempt to close the achievement gap, has added to the soft bigotry of low expectations. As stated earlier, attempts at accountability have done very little to encourage and improve the situation, and schools are as polarized as they have ever been. For instance, in 2012, the state of Florida rolled out some new accountability standards for both schools and teachers. Teacher evaluations would be partially calculated on a value-added model of student performance on state test scores. In a bargain to make this model fairer, the state board of education approved a six-year strategic plan with student-achievement goals that vary based on race, income, disability, and English proficiency. For example, Florida demanded that 86 percent of white students perform at or above grade level in mathematics, but for black students and Latino students, the goal was 74 percent achievement in mathematics (Isensee & Vasquez, 2012). This weighted calculation applied to all grade levels and all tested areas. Civil rights groups attacked and condemned the measures, but they illustrate how the magnitude of low academic expectations for traditionally margin-alized groups of students and communities is symptomatic of the victim mindset.

Conclusion

Movements develop from a burning desire to achieve a better life personally or for others. It requires discipline, passion, and a willing-ness to fight the external barriers to growth but more importantly to fight personal habits and barriers that prevent self-improvement. The historical, political, and economic barriers facing underperforming schools and students are real, and they are huge. However, remov-ing those external obstacles alone will not guarantee the closure of the achievement gap. An intense desire to work within the circle of influence (page 52) has to become the responsibility of the students, families, schools, and communities who want to close the achieve-ment gap once and for all.

CHAPTER 6

The Liberation Mindset

*Education either functions as an instrument which is
used to facilitate integration of the younger generation
into the logic of the present system and bring about
conformity or it becomes the practice of freedom, the
means by which men and women deal critically and
creatively with reality and discover how to participate
in the transformation of their world.*

—*Paulo Freire*

It is clear that the measures taken in the past to close the achievement gap have not worked. Many resources have been dedicated
to achieving the goal of academic equality in every public school,
but the gap still remains, and it is as large as it has ever been. So,
what will it take to close this stubborn gap? A change in mindset is
in order. As established in previous chapters, this change will not
be easy. There are people, communities, and systems that thrive off
the feeling and status associated with perceived superiority. There
are people, communities, and systems that feel comforted by the
ability to blame others for their current station instead of an intense
focus on self- and community improvement. The superiority and
victim mindsets serve everyone's interest except the students who
are caught in the middle.

Change will require a *liberation mindset*, which in turn will create liberating cultures that will properly serve all students—the type of cultures we should expect in a society that, by its founding document, identifies liberty as the right of every human being. The *liberation mindset* is an unwavering set of collective beliefs and actions rooted in the goal of achieving high levels of academic and social success for all students despite internal or external barriers. This chapter will lay out the important components of the liberation mindset, and I will provide case studies for each component. It will be apparent that these amazing schools and their shift in mindset and behaviors did not happen by accident; they were the product of a relentless commitment from school leaders with vision and focus.

Theories About the Liberation Mindset

If educators and community members believe that inequality is normal, then there is no theoretical foundation that can aggressively address the issue. The foundation of the liberation mindset is the belief that education is a right that all human beings share regardless of power or station in life. Social and political theorist Isaiah Berlin (1956) theorizes that humane societies operate under an assumption that equality is normal and therefore needs no justification and that inequality is abnormal and it needs to be justified and explained because it contradicts the basic nature of the human being.

This concept is captured in what is called *moral egalitarianism*, which is rooted in the belief that equality is central to the concept of justice. This philosophy is built on the foundation of six key principles (Gordon, 2015).

1. Unfair life circumstances should be equalized.
2. Equality is one of the most valuable products of justice.
3. General welfare should be increased by those who are able.
4. Justice is comparative.

5. Inequality is just when it destroys an advantage of one group over another in the pursuit of justice.

6. There are certain absolute human principles that are non-negotiable (such as freedom and human dignity).

In order to defeat the achievement gap that has plagued schools for years, educators have to operate under the assumption that inequality is abnormal and we are obligated to pursue equality in learning outcomes for our students if we believe in a fair and just society.

No force should be more passionate about pursuing change and progress than the people who would benefit most from the growth and improvement. Certainly, if student achievement outcomes improve significantly, educators, students, parents, and the community at large would benefit greatly.

This requires taking responsibility for factors Covey would deem to be within the circle of influence. It presents the best opportunity for rapid growth. When the circle of influence (factors within our control) expands, our circle of concern (things outside of our direct control) shrinks. The liberation mindset seeks to expand the circle of influence.

This is also achieved by fighting and advocating for the resources needed to improve one's station. An important component of the liberation mindset is advocacy. Educator and author Jonathan Kozol (1991) argues that the unequal distribution of resources for schools is the key reason we can predict achievement based upon race and class. As stated in chapter 1, racism and class bias are real. So, if moral egalitarianism is the philosophy that guides the liberation mindset, it would seem logical for schools and communities fighting for equality to lobby for their fair share of resources and opportunities. So, the belief in social justice should lead to social activism. Most major social shifts have been achieved through organized movements (such as voting rights, civil rights, and gay rights). Why should learning equality be any different? As Frederick Douglass states, "Power concedes nothing without a demand. It never has and it never will" (Douglass, 1857).

Components of the Liberation Mindset

The liberation mindset involves an unwavering commitment to a set of collective beliefs and actions rooted in the goal of achieving high levels of academic and social success for all students despite internal or external barriers. There are three main components of the liberation mindset.

1. **Equality:** Those with a liberation mindset believe that human potential is not a function of personal characteristics like race, gender, economic status, home language, national origin, or disability.

2. **Responsibility:** Those with a liberation mindset hold themselves as educators responsible for nurturing each student to his or her potential. They accept the responsibility of developing professional knowledge, practice, and systems to be responsive to the student population's needs.

3. **Advocacy:** Those with a liberation mindset believe that people and entities outside school must play an active and supportive role in the development of our students. They commit to hold others accountable for supporting their efforts to properly educate students through active participation, financial support, positive publicity, experiences, and legislation.

Schooling requires profound contributions from many people and leadership at all levels. People in the classroom, principal's office, central office, home, community, and in the legislative chambers, will be important in championing this mindset and organizing the policies and resources necessary to move from beliefs to actions. When it comes to leadership in changing mindsets and culture, school leadership, especially the principal's role, becomes very important in this endeavor. As Michael Usdan, Barbara McCloud, and Mary Podmostko (2000) from the Institute for Educational Leadership state, "The school principal is in the best position to change the important behaviors and habits of a school" (p. 7).

Schools that develop the liberation mindset do not view internal and external obstacles as insurmountable; they view them as challenges and opportunities for growth and to do what is perceived as impossible. They are egalitarian in their belief systems, and they possess superior professional skills. They recognize that students are not *at risk* but, as Yvette Jackson (2011) describes, *school dependent.* They believe that with the right guidance, resources, and enough time, all students can become academically and socially successful.

Equality

The first critical component of the liberation mindset is equality. It is critical to destroying the superiority mindset. Equality requires the collective belief that hierarchical systems are inhumane and counterproductive and they do not have a place in a public school with a diverse population of citizens. As explained in chapter 2, equality is the first principle in the U.S. Declaration of Independence, and nearly every public school references it in its mission and vision statements. So, equality is not a concept that people typically disagree with philosophically; the clash tends to happen more at a practical application level, when long-held assumptions and traditions are challenged. Egalitarian systems cannot be built in environments where educators believe that student achievement is based on a set of personal characteristics that determine whether learners will succeed. There are five indicators that help us examine whether a school is committed to equality.

1. We carefully monitor our student achievement data to ensure equity across all student groups, and we make adjustments to policies, practices, and procedures in response to those results to achieve greater levels of equity.

2. We carefully monitor our course offerings and academic program to ensure that we do not create a culturally or socioeconomically based caste system in relation to student enrollment in advanced or remedial coursework, and we adjust our policies, practices, and procedures to produce more equitable representation.

3. We carefully monitor our student engagement data to ensure equitable representation and to guard against bias. Some of the areas of monitoring include discipline data, attendance, extracurricular activity participation, and academic honor roll. We make adjustments to policies, practices, and procedures to achieve greater levels of equity.

4. We carefully monitor our school environment and learning material to ensure fair and equitable representation of cultural heritage, language, and economic background. We make adjustments to policies, practices, and resources to achieve greater levels of equity.

5. We carefully monitor parental involvement data to ensure equitable representation, especially in the areas of ethnic background and socioeconomic status. We make adjustments to our policies, practices, and procedures to achieve greater levels of equity.

To illustrate the fact that these behaviors are directly within the control of schools to achieve, I have highlighted a school that has made that commitment. In addition, I will provide some tangible results that prove that making this shift made a positive difference for students.

Case Study: Seneca High School (Louisville, Kentucky)

Seneca High School is a comprehensive high school in the Jefferson County Public Schools system in Louisville, Kentucky. Over the years, the school had developed a reputation of high achievement; they even boasted famous alumni like news anchorwoman Diane Sawyer and professional basketball Hall of Famer Wes Unseld. The school's reputation was sterling when it was racially and economically segregated, and the perception of excellence was largely due to the prevalence of the superiority mindset. However, the reputation of the school started to suffer when the student population changed over a twenty-year period, eventually resulting in the Kentucky Department of Education designating it as a persistently low-achieving school in 2010.

By 2014, Seneca had a very diverse student population. The school has an enrollment of over 1,400 students, and its population exhibits diversity in many different ways. Seventy-four percent of Seneca students are eligible to receive free or reduced school lunch because their parents earn an income below the national poverty line. Twenty-four percent of its students have limited English proficiency or are English learners. Thirteen percent of its student population is enrolled in special education. Its greatest level of diversity is in student ethnicity: 43 percent of Seneca students are black or African American, 42 percent are white, 11 percent are Latino, and 2 percent are Asian or Pacific Islanders (Kentucky Department of Education, 2014).

The high level of student diversity did not translate into a high level of academic and social equality according to the state report card on Seneca High School. Achievement gaps between students in advanced placement enrollment, state test scores, graduation rate, student discipline, and college and career readiness were huge for white and Asian students compared to black and Latino students.

In February 2011, Michelle Dillard was hired as the new principal charged with leading a school turnaround. In alignment with the accountability laws associated with a school identified as persistently low achieving, she replaced 38 percent of the teaching staff. School culture is complex, and it cannot be changed through simply replacing people; there has to be a change of mindset and behaviors, which in addition to replacing people is what Ms. Dillard and her team began to do.

Ms. Dillard assembled a Seneca turnaround team in the summer of 2011. The team was a mix of school administrators, support staff, and teacher leaders, and they completed a series of Kentucky Department of Education–organized professional development sessions. The team developed a turnaround plan that focused on three priority areas: (1) increasing overall academic performance, (2) transforming school culture, and (3) making data-informed decisions that promoted equity.

To provide clarity of focus, the team collectively recreated the school mission and vision statements, and each staff member was required to memorize and publicly state the mission statement before professional meetings (which the team renamed *learning opportunities*). In developing the school's collective focus and commitments, Ms. Dillard led a review of what she called the brutal facts and the beautiful facts. The data showed that there were large disparities in both mathematics and reading for white and nonwhite students, and there was an equally large graduation rate disparity between the same groups. On the other hand, the review of survey data found that students and staff really liked the school and took pride in teaching and learning in that environment, even though the results were not stellar. The review of these data and the discussion of the beliefs, attitudes, policies, and practices that produced them were very revealing for the teachers and leadership team. They decided that if they were committed to equality, their belief systems and behaviors needed to change. As a result of having the courage to collectively address the elephants in the room, they were able to create a mission and vision that would guide their collective beliefs and behaviors. Seneca's mission is as follows: "The mission of Seneca High School is to prepare students for college and career goals as measured by state academic standards. We are committed to providing an environment and a system of support to ensure all students are successful" (Seneca High School, n.d.), and the vision states, "Seneca High School is a positive, caring community where staff members and students are committed to becoming an exemplary model for success in a global society" (Seneca High School, n.d.).

Creating a mission and a vision is not enough to close the achievement gap. But the principal and the school turnaround team were committed to keeping the philosophies that the staff collectively developed and committed to at the forefront of their thoughts and conversations. In addition to the school's explicit focus and direction, the team also agreed to change its language. At Seneca High School, students are referred to as *scholars*, and educational professionals are referred to as *champions*. The team understood, though, that creating a healthy culture requires more than philosophical agreement and a change in terminology; it requires policies and practices that support the collective and egalitarian philosophy.

To ensure that the mission and vision were actively guiding behavior and practice, the school built and monitored critical systems. The first critical system required all professional staff members to become a part of a collaborative team. The collaborative teacher teams were required to answer the four critical questions of a PLC, identified in the preface (pages xiv–xv) to this book, that focus on curriculum alignment, common formative assessments, systematic academic intervention, and systematic academic enrichment. The teams were required to compare student growth against a standard level of learning proficiency and identify current student proficiency with one of three colors: red indicated that a student was far below the standard, yellow indicated that the student was close to proficiency on a learning target, and green meant that a student had met the learning target. The collaborative team of teachers would respond to its data with tangible intervention or enrichment strategies. An administrator was present at each meeting to ensure teacher focus during collaboration and to provide administrative support for teachers as needed. Each team was required to create measurable goals, which focused on raising the academic bar for all students and closing gaps in achievement. Other school professionals, like counselors, met regularly and reviewed data and worked to close gaps in areas like attendance, behavior, and enrollment in rigorous courses.

Equality in academic skill development is the first priority at Seneca, but equality in opportunity is important as well. In response to a huge ethnic and socioeconomic gap in the students enrolled in advanced placement classes, Seneca adopted an open-enrollment policy so that any student who wanted to enroll in an advanced placement course could choose to do so, instead of past policy which required a relatively high student grade point average and teacher recommendation. Secondly, it implemented a program called *college connection* to expose every Seneca student to the dispositions, skills, and attitudes necessary to enroll in and earn a degree from a postsecondary institution after graduating from high school. A freshman academy was developed at the ninth-grade level that organized teachers and students into small learning communities. Each common group of teachers shared a common group of students and created a smaller, tighter-knit environment that allowed students and teachers to create powerful personal relationships to increase the likelihood of graduation.

It would be less than genuine to claim that the change in mindset and policies was easy. It took relentless focus and sacrifice from a visionary administration and turnaround team and the courage of the school Believers who were willing to stand up and advocate for equality both publically and privately. One anonymous Seneca teacher writes:

> We've learned how to focus our conversations on the four critical questions of a PLC; how to develop effective intervention systems, and how to transform our culture into a healthier, more student-centered place of learning. Our staff is hardworking, dedicated, and committed to student achievement. This did not come without a price. We battled resistance both internally and externally and, at times, it seemed easier to give up and return to status quo. But, the fight was worth it, and I am looking forward to our future and what we can become. (personal communication, May 8, 2014)

The results of Seneca's transformation have been remarkable. In 2011, the state of Kentucky determined only 34 percent of Seneca students were college and career ready. By 2013, that number had increased to 48.8 percent. That number included a growth of 21.77 percent for African American students and 19.2 percent for English learners. The graduation rate for Seneca students grew from just 59.7 percent to 84.2 percent during Ms. Dillard's tenure as principal between 2011 and 2013. Finally, between the years 2010 to 2013, Seneca's performance on state assessments and achievement indicators for the state of Kentucky grew from being ranked in the bottom 5 percent of Kentucky high schools to the 42 percentile of achievement in just three years (Kentucky Department of Education, 2014).

The Kentucky Department of Education conducted its leadership assessment of priority schools in 2013 and awarded Seneca High School with the Powerful Practice commendation (Kentucky Department of Education and AdvancED, 2013), stating, "Educators at Seneca High School are commended for their efforts to create instructionally based professional learning communities in support of teaching and learning through the school" (p. 15).

Responsibility

The second critical component of the liberation mindset is responsibility. Responsibility involves the belief that the school and its employees are accountable for students' development, and the belief that they have the collective efficacy necessary to develop an egalitarian learning environment. The principle of responsibility is not solely restricted to the educators; they work together to develop this principle in the lives and behaviors of students and parents as well.

Psychologists Angela Lee Duckworth and Lauren Eskreis-Winkler (2013) use the term *grit* to describe the responsibility necessary to develop a liberating learning environment. Grit is the persistence over time to overcome challenges and accomplish big goals (Duckworth & Eskreis-Winkler, 2013). Many educators have begun to believe that improvements in instruction, curriculum, and school environments are simply not enough to raise the achievement of all learners, especially disadvantaged ones—grit is necessary as well. Grit comprises a suite of traits and behaviors, including:

- Goal-directedness (knowing where to go and how to get there)
- Motivation (having a strong will to achieve identified goals)
- Self-control (avoiding distractions and focusing on the task at hand)
- Positive mindset (embracing challenge and viewing failure as a learning opportunity)

Schools that want to eliminate the achievement gap have to develop a sense of grit and persistence. This process starts with the professionals and grows to include students and parents. We cannot allow disadvantaged students to develop a sense of learned helplessness that will make them victims forever. Someone or something has to break the cycle of underachievement. There are six indicators that help us determine if a school has developed responsibility.

1. We have an unwavering focus and commitment to universal student achievement, and we will not stop experimenting and innovating until we achieve that goal.

2. We develop an unwavering focus and commitment to high achievement in our students and parents, and we will not stop experimenting and innovating until we achieve that goal.

3. We monitor and disaggregate student achievement and engagement data and strategically use our professional development resources and time to address professional skill development in high-need areas.

4. We monitor and disaggregate student achievement and engagement data to strategically develop policies and systems to support and develop struggling students.

5. We refrain from using negative and pessimistic language when collaborating about high-need students and families.

6. Our physical school environment reflects and displays the best qualities of our students and community, and we use it to encourage our students and families to strive for excellence.

Responsibility has traditionally been viewed as a function of the home and the greater society. When students are in a disadvantaged situation (suffering from racial stereotypes or the trials of poverty), this trait can be developed at school. I am not just proposing teaching personal responsibility for students, I am also proposing that educational professionals take responsibility for student learning as it relates to the policies, practices, and procedures implemented within the walls of the school. Kendrick Middle School is an example of how this principle can be put into action.

Case Study: Kendrick Middle School (Jonesboro, Georgia)

Kendrick Middle School is a grades 6–8 school in the Clayton County Public Schools near Atlanta, Georgia. The student population of Kendrick Middle School is very different than the diverse population at Seneca High School. According to the school report card from the Clayton County Public Schools (2013), Kendrick has an enrollment of 847 students, and 78 percent of the students are African American, 17 percent are Latino, 2 percent are Asian, and 2 percent are white. The report also indicates that 91.5 percent of Kendrick students live at or below the national poverty line. The student profile of this school would lead a person with a superiority mindset or victim mindset to believe that student achievement would be low. These reports reflect a very different reality.

The same school report card indicates that Kendrick Middle School made phenomenal growth in student achievement on the Georgia academic assessment tools. According to the Clayton County Public Schools (2013), between 2006 and 2013, Kendrick sixth graders' reading proficiency grew from 77.6 percent to 91.3 percent; seventh graders' reading proficiency grew from 65 percent to 92.1 percent; and eighth graders' reading proficiency grew from 86.5 percent to 95.1 percent. There was also phenomenal growth in mathematics between 2006 and 2013. Kendrick sixth graders' proficiency grew from 48.6 percent to 76.8 percent; seventh graders' proficiency grew from 72.4 percent to 86.6 percent; and eighth graders' proficiency grew from 71.9 percent to 79.9 percent. The most impressive statistic came from the state science exam. In 2013, 100 percent of Kendrick students tested in science met or exceeded state science standards compared to 82.7 percent of the students in the state of Georgia meeting or exceeding state standards in science.

What was the catalyst for this extraordinary school turnaround? According to the school's principal, Marcus Jackson, it was an intense focus on student development at the academic and personal levels. Jackson believed that with the proper guidance, all students can and will strive for excellence. As school principal, he believed it was his responsibility to develop the mindset and the systems that would provide students with the proper academic and personal guidance (M. Jackson, personal communication, November 7, 2014).

One of the pivotal programs the administration and staff implemented at Kendrick Middle School is the Core Value Program. The purpose of the Core Value Program is to empower and educate students with practical life skills, responsible behavior, and positive peer influence through activities that build grit. The staff meet every Wednesday with a focus on the month's core value. The teachers have agreed to implement that core value into every lesson and review and discuss with their students every day. Periodically, the school invites local business owners, coaches, and other community members to assist in positively developing and directing Kendrick students.

The Core Value Program focuses on important personal development traits like honesty, integrity, respect, and perseverance (M. Jackson, personal communication, November 7, 2014). These are areas where educators have traditionally relied on parents to produce. At Kendrick, they believe that they have to share that responsibility, because ultimately the student suffers if not properly addressed. The school leadership team developed the Core Value Program after strategically analyzing the school performance data and finding very specific areas of need that were directly related to school and student habits and conduct. Instead of complaining about the data, the team chose to act. Mr. Jackson reported that participating in schoolwide efforts to improve student achievement is not optional at Kendrick; it is a part of teachers' and administrators' professional duty, and he feels responsible for holding both the staff and students accountable for solving problems that are directly within their influence.

Advocacy

The third critical component of the liberation mindset is advocacy. If equality is important in a democratic society, then everyone must receive his or her fair share of the resources. Advocacy is based on the belief that we can have influence outside of our direct control, and we are obligated to collaborate with others in our attempt to create equitable learning opportunities for all students. As described in chapter 1, the government has made several attempts to close funding and opportunity gaps for students, but those gaps still exist. In 2008, the Chicago Public Schools received $10,400 from the state to educate each student while neighboring districts like New Trier Township received $17,000 per student, and Sunset Ridge received $16,000 per student (Sadovi, Malone, & Black, 2008).

This problem of resource allocation and equal opportunity is not just isolated to one state or region—it is a national problem, and it exists in every state (Allen, 1997). Parents who lack political, social, and economic capital find it hard to secure the best opportunities, facilities, and resources that their children need to compete in today's world. Schools that truly embrace the liberation mindset find that it is a part of their duty and responsibility to secure the best resources and opportunities for the students they serve. There are five indicators that help us assess whether a school has developed advocacy.

1. We empower students and parents with information about resources available to them both inside and outside school that promote academic and personal development.

2. We are politically involved as a school unit or in cooperation with an agency or organization to lobby our board of education, state legislature, and federal legislature to pass policies and laws that benefit our students.

3. We educate our parents and community about opportunities and resources available to them to influence local, state, and federal policies that impact our students.

4. We organize to create partnerships with outside agencies to provide additional resources and opportunities for our students' academic and personal development.

5. We actively publicize and highlight the achievements of our students, staff, and parents to create a sense of pride and goodwill for our school.

Students need adult advocates to have a fair shot at a bright future. Children who have politically and financially savvy parents tend to benefit from the advantages that their parents create for them. But kids without parents with profound economic and political influence need adults at home and school to work together to make sure that they get their fair share of resources and opportunities. Martin Luther King Jr. Elementary School in Hanford, California, is a great example of this form of advocacy.

Case Study: Martin Luther King Jr. Elementary (Hanford, California)

Martin Luther King Jr. Elementary School is located in the Central Valley region of California in Hanford, California, which is nearly forty miles outside of Fresno. Hanford is a rural community of just over 53,000 citizens. The school is a part of the Hanford Elementary School District, which serves students in grades preK–8. The school district webpage provides a report card for each of its schools, and King's demographic data indicate that the school has a student population that is predominantly Latino and impoverished. King has nearly four hundred students, of which 83 percent are Latino, 9 percent are white, 5 percent are African American, and 3 percent are Asian. The state reports that 77 percent of students enrolled at King are not native English speakers (California Department of Education, 2014). Like the other two schools featured in this chapter, there is a high level of family poverty. Eighty-seven percent of the students at King live in homes with an average income below the national poverty line (Martin Luther King Jr. Elementary School, 2014). Again, a person with a superiority mindset or a victim mindset might assume that students at King perform poorly on nearly all measures of student achievement based on their demographics.

The state of California measures its schools' progress through a formula called the academic performance index (API). API is a single number that the California Department of Education assigns to each school to measure overall school performance and improvement over time on statewide testing. The API ranges from 200 to 1,000, with 800 as the state goal for all schools. In 2010, King Elementary had an API score of 746, and by 2013, the API was 806 (California Department of Education, 2014). How did this school with a high-minority, high-poverty, and large English learner population exceed the state's expectations for all schools? It organized to become the students' biggest advocates.

Debra Colvard, who has served as the school's principal since 2005, leads King Elementary. The low student expectations of the staff, parents, and community personally and professionally disturbed Ms. Colvard. In 2009, she and the staff at King decided to collaborate and change their school's trajectory, and they created the MLK Vision for Student Success (D. Colvard, personal communication, May 9, 2014).

The MLK Vision for Student Success was a collaborative effort aimed at strategically addressing the most vital needs of King students through a partnership between students, educators, parents, and the community. The vision organized the improvement efforts into five key areas: (1) numeracy and literacy, (2) cognitive development and critical thinking, (3) career exploration, (4) character development, and (5) parental and community involvement. A team of educators, parents, and community members led each key area and served as the central decision makers for the school's improvement efforts in those specific areas. The team members were not just committed to analyzing the problem; they were all committed to becoming active learners and collectively seeking best practice in their area of influence. Each team created a set of measurable annual goals and met two times per month to strategize and implement innovative programs.

The character development team was essential to creating the right environment for students to thrive. According to Ms. Colvard, prior to creating the MLK Vision for Student Success, students were regularly defiant and violent (D. Colvard, personal communication, May 9, 2014). Instead of blaming the victim, the character development team decided to do some research on the causes of student defiance, anger, and low self-esteem. Team members were shocked to discover that students' behaviors were a manifestation of how they were socialized at home, in the community, and at school. The team created a seven-step program that blended personal strategies, parental strategies, community service, and outside agency intervention for students with the greatest needs. The result has been a drastic change in student confidence and academic focus. One team member states, "Our connection to the community became stronger as we brought the students into the community to be served and to serve others" (Teacher, personal communication, May 9, 2014). The character development team solicited volunteer hours from community members and parents to mentor students, and it secured several donations from local businesses and citizens to fund their initiatives for students.

Because of its collaboration and advocacy, King Elementary is highly celebrated. In 2013, the school received special recognition from its state representative in honor of its English learners' academic progress. The *Hanford Sentinel*, the local newspaper, featured the school's growth and community impact in 2011 (Santiago, 2011). The school staff members have also presented their work at several local and national conferences as a model of school turnaround.

Diagnostic Tools for Developing a Liberation Mindset

Self-reflection is a very important process for an individual or an institution that has committed to change and transformation. Improvement occurs when there is a deep commitment to grow and a willingness to look in the mirror. If schools are going to change their mindsets, and eventually change their culture, the practitioners have to be willing to do some deep diagnostic work. This process can be intimidating, and we often don't like, or try to disprove, what the mirror tells us. However, better service for millions of students will be the result of this sacrifice.

In the 21st century context of schooling, self-reflection is scarier than it has ever been in the history of our profession. Government has misused assessment and turned it into a weapon instead of a diagnostic tool (Melago, 2008). I have found in my experience working with thousands of schools and educators that their defensiveness stems from fear that the school district, community, state, or federal government will judge or scorn them (and given their experience with standardized tests and school ratings, that sentiment is understandable). A 2005 study of school turnaround reveals that "improvement is impossible without tools to diagnose performance and a system to analyze and make decisions based upon objective information" (Petrides & Nodine, 2005, p. 22).

To assist schools in strategically developing their mindset and culture for improvement, I have developed two sets of diagnostic tools to assess their current reality and to make decisions according to the assessment results. If we are going to make progress, we first have to be aware of our starting point. The first set of tools (figures 6.1–6.3, pages 110–115) includes schoolwide surveys that all major stakeholders can fill out, including professional staff, clerical and classified staff, administration, students, and parents. The survey tools assess people's thoughts and perceptions. They will give you a good look at the organization's mindset. The second set of tools (figures 6.4–6.6, pages 116–121) includes four-point rubrics that will require the assessor (preferably an administrator) to gather information to assess the organization's systems and structures. These tools are helpful in determining what we do as opposed to what we believe. The combination of both sets of information should help the strategic school move closer to having a liberation mindset and achieving high levels of learning for all students. Visit **go.solution-tree.com/leadership** for reproducible versions of these figures.

Conclusion

The tools that would allow us to achieve academic equity in schools have been at our disposal for years. Our greatest problem has been developing the will to implement the strategies and create the mindset and culture necessary to properly utilize them. The liberation mindset allows us a unique opportunity to fulfill the promise of egalitarianism in public schools. Change will require personal and institutional commitment, and I do not pretend that it is an easy process. The principles of the liberation mindset will provide students, educators, parents, and communities with a map that will guide them to improvement as opposed to being lost in despair.

1: Strongly Disagree   2: Disagree   3: Neutral   4: Agree   5: Strongly Agree

Statement	1	2	3	4	5
We carefully monitor our student achievement data to ensure equity across all student groups, and we make adjustments to policies, practices, and procedures in response to those results to achieve greater levels of equity.					
We are alarmed when our student achievement data are not equitable.					
Our collaborative meetings are student centered and focused on equity.					
We make changes to our practice when our data are disproportionate.					
We carefully monitor our course offerings and academic program to ensure that we do not create a culturally or socioeconomically based caste system in relation to student enrollment in advanced or remedial coursework, and we adjust our policies, practices, and procedures to produce more equitable representation.					
We have created a fair process that allows all students to pursue advanced coursework.					
It bothers us when advanced or remedial courses have skewed student representation.					
Our assessment system is fair and free of cultural or socioeconomic bias.					
We believe that students have a fair opportunity to achieve in our school.					
We carefully monitor our student engagement data to ensure equitable representation and to guard against bias. Some of the areas of monitoring include discipline data, attendance, extracurricular activity participation, and academic honor roll. (*continued*)					
Our discipline procedures are fair and do not reflect cultural or economic bias.					
We are alarmed when inequitable discipline data are identified.					
Our attendance procedures are fair and do not reflect cultural or economic bias.					

We make adjustments to policies, practices, and procedures to achieve greater levels of equity.	We are alarmed when student recognition is not equitable.						
	We make adjustments to our student engagement policies when there is statistical evidence of inequality for one group compared to the norm.						
We carefully monitor our school environment and learning material to ensure fair and equitable representation of cultural heritage, language, and economic background. We make adjustments to policies, practices, and resources to achieve greater levels of equity.	Our teaching material is culturally and economically diverse.						
	We use methods that respect all cultural and economic backgrounds.						
	We seek professional development opportunities that help us become more culturally responsive in our practice.						
We carefully monitor parental involvement data to ensure equitable representation, especially in the areas of ethnic background and socioeconomic status. We make adjustments to our policies, practices, and procedures to achieve greater levels of equity.	We reach out to all parents and make an honest attempt to involve all parents in school decisions and activities.						
	We build systems that make the process of parent engagement easy and inviting.						
	We make adjustments to our behavior when our data inform us that parent involvement is disproportionate.						

Figure 6.1: Survey for assessing perceptions about equality.

Visit go.solution-tree.com/leadership for a reproducible version of this figure.

1: Strongly Disagree 2: Disagree 3: Neutral 4: Agree 5: Strongly Agree	1	2	3	4	5
We have an unwavering focus and commitment to universal student achievement, and we will not stop experimenting and innovating until we achieve that goal.	Our collaborative conversations are egalitarian, and we focus on student achievement.				
	We use data and feedback as tools for growth, and they strengthen our commitment to student achievement.				
	We make adjustments to our practice when necessary to achieve greater levels of achievement.				
We develop an unwavering focus and commitment to high achievement in our students and parents, and we will not stop experimenting and innovating until we achieve that goal.	We have high expectations of achievement for all our students.				
	We demand that students continue to practice until they accomplish mastery.				
	We develop perseverance and grit in our students.				
We monitor and disaggregate student achievement and engagement data and strategically use our professional development resources and time to address professional skill development in the high-need areas.	We believe that it is our responsibility to be responsive to student needs.				
	We believe that developing student responsibility for mastery of their own learning is partially our responsibility.				
	We seek opportunities to help us grow professionally when we feel that we cannot meet a student need.				

We monitor and disaggregate student achievement and engagement data to strategically develop policies and systems to support and develop struggling students.	We believe that student content mastery is our responsibility.					
	We believe that developing student confidence and character is partially our responsibility.					
	We develop systems that respond to specific student needs.					
We refrain from using negative and pessimistic language when collaborating about high-need students and families.	We refrain from using negative or defamatory language in our informal and formal interactions.					
	We are willing to confront our colleagues' negative attitudes or behaviors.					
Our physical school environment reflects and displays the best qualities of our students and community, and we use it to encourage our students and families to strive for excellence.	We believe that we are responsible for displaying symbols and artifacts that positively reinforce our values and build student confidence.					
	We recognize student strengths both formally and informally in our practice and environment.					

Figure 6.2: Survey for assessing perceptions about responsibility.

Visit go.solution-tree.com/leadership for a reproducible version of this figure.

1: Strongly Disagree 2: Disagree 3: Neutral 4: Agree 5: Strongly Agree	1	2	3	4	5
We empower students and parents with information about resources available to them both inside and outside school that promote academic and personal development.					
We view students as powerful advocates for their own success, and we provide opportunities for them to advocate for themselves and to be an active participant in a democratic school process.					
We view parents as powerful advocates for their child's success, and we provide opportunities for them to advocate.					
We communicate with parents about political, economic, and educational issues that affect their children, and we view them as a powerful lobby.					
We are politically involved as a school unit or in cooperation with an agency or organization to lobby our board of education, state legislature, and federal legislature to pass policies and laws that benefit our students.					
We actively lobby and influence local, state, and federal officials to secure the resources and conditions necessary for optimal student growth.					
We believe that we are powerful and influential, and we have the efficacy necessary to change systems.					
We support causes and agencies that advance our collective purpose.					

We educate our parents and community about opportunities and resources available to them to influence local, state, and federal policies that impact our students.							
We communicate with parents with the intent of empowering them.							
We encourage our parents to be active advocates for their children in the area of resource allocation and favorable policy.							
We organize to create partnerships with outside agencies to provide additional resources and opportunities for our students' academic and personal development.							
We actively seek resources and opportunities for our students by partnering with outside agencies.							
We believe that we share in the responsibility to create powerful life experiences for students.							
We are resourceful, and we do not let limitations stop our drive for universal student achievement.							
We actively publicize and highlight the achievements of our students, staff, and parents to create a sense of pride and goodwill for our school.							
We believe that it is our responsibility to inform the public about the great things happening in our school.							
We communicate regularly with the local media to create positive press for our school.							
We prominently display positive press or student accomplishments around our school.							

Figure 6.3: Survey for assessing perceptions about advocacy.

Visit go.solution-tree.com/leadership for a reproducible version of this figure.

Equality: Collective belief that hierarchical systems are inhumane and counterproductive and they do not have a place in a public school with a diverse population of citizens

4 **Exemplary Level of Development and Implementation**	Achievement disparities exist between student groups, especially poor and minority students, we have implemented a strategic plan, and there is longitudinal evidence that the gaps are closing. Poor or minority students are underrepresented in the measures of high achievement, we have implemented a strategic plan, and there is longitudinal evidence that the gaps are closing. Poor or minority students are overrepresented in negative discipline and attendance data, we have implemented a strategic plan, and there is longitudinal evidence that the gaps are closing.
3 **Fully Functional and Operational Level of Development and Implementation**	Achievement disparities exist between student groups, especially poor and minority students, we have implemented a strategic plan, but there is limited evidence of success. Poor or minority students are underrepresented in the measures of high achievement, and we have implemented a strategic plan, but there is limited evidence of success. Poor or minority students are overrepresented in negative discipline and attendance data, and we have implemented a strategic plan, but there is limited evidence of success.
2 **Limited Development or Partial Implementation**	Achievement disparities exist between student groups, especially poor and minority students, and we have developed a strategic plan but not effectively implemented it. Poor or minority students are underrepresented in the measures of high achievement, and we have developed a strategic plan but not effectively implemented it. Poor or minority students are overrepresented in negative discipline and attendance data, and we have developed a strategic plan but not effectively implemented it.

1 Little to No Development and Implementation	Achievement disparities exist between student groups, especially poor and minority students, and there is no strategic plan to address the disparities.
	Poor or minority students are underrepresented in the measures of high achievement, and there is no strategic plan to address the issue.
	Poor or minority students are overrepresented in negative discipline and attendance data, and there is no strategic plan to address the issue.
	Supporting evidence used: ☐ State test scores ☐ Formative assessment data ☐ Student discipline and attendance data ☐ Student grade distribution ☐ Requirements for advanced coursework ☐ School handbook and code of conduct ☐ Master course schedule ☐ Instructional and resource material ☐ School décor and aesthetics ☐ Other _____

Figure 6.4: Rubric for assessing equality.

Visit go.solution-tree.com/leadership for a reproducible version of this figure.

Responsibility: Belief that the school and its employees are accountable for the development of its students, and the belief that staff have the collective efficacy necessary to develop an egalitarian learning environment

4 **Exemplary Level of Development and Implementation**	We identify and recognize student gaps in the areas of background knowledge and academic skill, we have implemented a plan to address these issues, and we have evidence of longitudinal growth.	We identify and recognize gaps in student social skills and personal experience, and we have implemented a plan to address these issues, and we have evidence of longitudinal growth.	We recognize that we have difficulty instructing and building relationships with students from cultures different than our own. We have implemented a plan of action and received professional development, and we have evidence of longitudinal growth.
3 **Fully Functional and Operational Level of Development and Implementation**	We identify and recognize student gaps in the areas of background knowledge and academic skill, and we have implemented a plan to address these issues, but there has been limited growth.	We identify and recognize gaps in student social skills and personal experience, and we have implemented a plan to address these issues, but there has been limited growth.	We recognize that we have difficulty instructing and building relationships with students from cultures different than our own. We have implemented a plan of action and received professional development, but there has been limited growth and progress.
2 **Limited Development or Partial Implementation**	We identify and recognize student gaps in the areas of background knowledge and academic skill, and we have developed a plan to address these issues, but it has not been implemented.	We identify and recognize gaps in student social skills and personal experience, and we have developed a plan to address these issues, but it has not been implemented.	We recognize that we have difficulty instructing and building relationships with students from cultures different than our own. We have developed a plan of action and received professional development, but there is no implementation.

1 Little to No Development and Implementation	We identify and recognize student gaps in the areas of background knowledge and academic skill, but there is no strategic plan to address these issues.
	We identify and recognize gaps in student social skills and personal experiences, but there is no strategic plan to address these issues.
	We recognize that we have difficulty instructing and building relationships with students from cultures different than our own, but there is no strategic plan or professional development devoted to solving the problem.

Supporting evidence used:

☐ State test scores

☐ Formative assessment data

☐ Student discipline and attendance data

☐ Student grade distribution

☐ School mission and vision

☐ School-improvement plan

☐ Classroom walkthroughs and observations

☐ School handbook and code of conduct

☐ Parent and student surveys

☐ Collaborative team–meeting notes

☐ Other _____

Figure 6.5: Rubric for assessing responsibility.

Visit go.solution-tree.com/leadership for a reproducible version of this figure.

Advocacy: Belief that we can have influence outside of our direct control and we are obligated to collaborate with others in our attempt to create equitable learning opportunities for all students

4 **Exemplary Level of Development and Implementation**	We recognize that our school and students are resource poor. We have a strategic plan, and we meet student and school needs at every important level. We recognize that our parents are resource poor, and we collaborate with them to empower them personally, educationally, and politically. We recognize that district, state, and federal policies adversely affect our students and our school. We collaborate and develop an effective counterproposal, and we secure influence through membership or collaboration with other groups or agencies.
3 **Fully Functional and Operational Level of Development and Implementation**	We recognize that our school and students are resource poor. We have a strategic plan, but we only partially secure our needs. We recognize that our parents are resource poor, but we only collaborate with them on nonthreatening and nonessential issues. We recognize that district, state, and federal policies adversely affect our students and our school. We collaborate and develop an effective counterproposal, but we do not secure the support of other stakeholders, such as parents and community members, to leverage political pressure to ensure that policymakers consider our plan.
2 **Limited Development or Partial Implementation**	We recognize that our school and students are resource poor. We have a strategic plan, but we do not fully implement it. We recognize that our parents are resource poor, but we only collaborate with them when problems arise. We recognize that district, state, and federal policies adversely affect our students and our school. We collaborate internally, but we do not present an effective case to local, state, or federal officials.

1 **Little to No Development and Implementation**	We recognize that our school and students are resource poor, but there is no strategic plan to address the issues. We recognize that our parents are resource poor, but we do not collaborate with them to address the issues. We recognize that district, state, and federal policies adversely affect our students and our school, but we do not organize to lobby for better conditions.
	Supporting evidence used: ❑ School budget ❑ School staffing allocation ❑ School-improvement plan ❑ Collective bargaining agreement ❑ Enrichment and extracurricular offerings ❑ School technology and equipment ❑ Field trip and field experience opportunities ❑ External partnerships ❑ Labor and political affiliations ❑ Parent-teacher organization or parent-teacher association ❑ Media publicity ❑ Other _____

Figure 6.6: Rubric for assessing advocacy.

Visit go.solution-tree.com/leadership for a reproducible version of this figure.

References and Resources

Academic Benchmarks. (2014). *Common Core State Standards adoption map.* Accessed at www.academicbenchmarks.com/ccss -state-status on May 16, 2014.

Akey, T. M. (2006). *School context, student attitudes and behavior, and academic achievement: An exploratory analysis.* New York: Manpower Demonstration Research Corporation.

Alexander, M. (2012). *The new Jim Crow: Mass incarceration in the age of colorblindness.* New York: New Press.

Allen, J. (1997, May 2). Inequity in funding of public education raises justice issues. *National Catholic Reporter.* Accessed at http:// natcath.org/NCR_Online/archives2/1997b/050297/050297a .htm on November 10, 2014.

Anderson, N. (2010, January 28). Administration pushes to rework No Child Left Behind law. *The Washington Post.* Accessed at www.washingtonpost.com/wp-dyn/content/article/2010/01/26 /AR2010012604586.html on November 10, 2014.

Annie E. Casey Foundation. (2011). *The 2011 Kids Count data book: State profiles of child well-being.* Accessed at www.aecf.org /resources/2011-kids-count-data-book on November 10, 2014.

Apuzzo, M. (2014). Holder and Republicans unite to soften sentencing laws. *The New York Times.* Accessed at www.nytimes .com/2014/03/04/us/politics/holder-and-republicans-unite-to -soften-sentencing-laws.html?hp&_r=0 on April 13, 2015.

Arciniega, T. A. (1977). The challenge of multicultural education for teacher educators. *Journal of Research and Development in Education, 11*(1), 52–69.

Arizona House Bill 2281, 49th Legislature 2nd Regular (2010).

August, D., Goldenberg, C., & Rueda, R. (2010). Restrictive state language policies: Are they scientifically based? In P. Gándara & M. Hopkins (Eds.), *Forbidden language: English learners and restrictive language policies* (pp. 139–158). New York: Teachers College Press.

Austin, G., & Johnson, D. (2012). Hispanic or Latino: Which is correct? *Profiles in Diversity Journal*. Accessed at www .diversityjournal.com/9724-hispanic-or-latino-which-is-correct on May 5, 2014.

Baker, P., & Dillon, S. (2010, February 22). Obama pitches education proposal to governors. *The New York Times*. Accessed at www.nytimes.com/2010/02/23/education/23educ.html?_r=0 on November 10, 2014.

Bean, F. D., & Tienda, M. (1987). *The Hispanic population of the United States*. New York: SAGE.

Berlin, I. (1956). Equality as an ideal. *Proceedings of the Aristotelian Society, 61*, 301–326.

Bloom, B. S. (1981). *All our children learning: A primer for parents, teachers, and other educators*. New York: McGraw-Hill.

Bowles, S., & Gintis, H. (1976). *Schooling in capitalist America: Educational reform and the contradictions of economic life*. New York: Basic Books.

Bowles, S., & Gintis, H. (2011). *Schooling in capitalist America: Educational reform and the contradictions of economic life* (Rev. ed.). Chicago: Haymarket Books.

Brinton, C. (1938). *The anatomy of revolution*. New York: Norton.

Brown, S. R., & Chapman, B. (2014, September 2). Exclusive: 90 city schools failed to pass a single black or Hispanic student on state tests, study shows. *New York Daily News*. Accessed at www .nydailynews.com/new-york/education/exclusive-achievement -gap-worsens-black-hispanic-students-article-1.1924366 on November 10, 2014.

Brown v. Board of Educ., 347 U.S. 483 (1954)

Burnham, T. C., & Johnson, D. D. P. (2005). The biological and evolutionary logic of human cooperation. *Analyze and Kritik, 27,* 113–135.

Burrell, T. (2010). *Brainwashed: Challenging the myth of black inferiority* (3rd ed.). Carlsbad, CA: SmileyBooks.

Calefati, J. (2010, May 12). Arizona bans ethnic studies. *Mother Jones.* Accessed at www.motherjones.com/mojo/2010/05/ethnic-studies-banned-arizona on May 5, 2014.

California Department of Education. (2014). *API reports.* Accessed at www.cde.ca.gov/ta/ac/ap/apireports.asp on May 12, 2014.

Carpenter, C. (2011, March 31). WNC teachers to Shuler: NCLB must be fixed or nixed. *Macon County News.* Accessed at www.maconnews.com/news/education/629-wnc-teachers-to-shuler-nclb-must-be-fixed-or-nixed on November 10, 2014.

Carson, C., & Holloran, P. (Eds.). (1998). *A knock at midnight: Inspiration from the great sermons of reverend Martin Luther King, Jr.* New York: Warner Books. Accessed at http://mlk-kpp01.stanford.edu/index.php/kingpapers/article/remaining_awake_through_a_great_revolution on January 8, 2015.

Chakrabarti, R., & Setren, E. (2011, December). *The impact of the Great Recession on school district finances: Evidence from New York* (Staff Report No. 534). New York: Federal Reserve Bank of New York. Accessed at www.newyorkfed.org/research/staff_reports/sr534.pdf on April 9, 2015.

Chiodo, A. J., Hernández-Murillo, R., & Owyang, M. T. (2010). Nonlinear effects of school quality on house prices. *Federal Reserve Bank of St. Louis Review, 92*(3), 185–204.

Clayton County Public Schools. (2013). *2011–2012 Accountability report card, Kendrick Middle School.* Jonesboro, GA: Author.

Clotfelter, C., Ladd, H. F., Vigdor, J., & Wheeler, J. (2006). *High poverty schools and the distribution of teachers and principals* (Working Paper No. 1). Washington, DC: Urban Institute, National Center for Analysis of Longitudinal Data in Education Research.

Cole, C. (2009). *Performing South Africa's Truth Commission: Stages of transition.* Bloomington, IN: Indiana University Press.

Collins, J. (2001). *Good to great: Why some companies make the leap . . . and others don't.* New York: Harper Business.

Connell, R. W. (1993). *Schools and social justice.* Philadelphia: Temple University Press.

Cotton, K. (1989). *Expectations and student outcomes* (School Improvement Research Series, close-up #7). Portland, OR: Northwest Regional Educational Laboratory.

Covey, S. R. (1989). *The 7 habits of highly effective people: Powerful lessons in personal change.* New York: Simon & Schuster.

Cummins, J. (2000). *Language, power and pedagogy: Bilingual children in the crossfire.* Tonawanda, NY: Multilingual Matters.

Davis, K., & Moore, W. E. (1945). Some principles of stratification. *American Sociological Review, 10*(2), 242–249.

Deal, T. E., & Peterson, K. D. (1999). *Shaping school culture: The heart of leadership.* San Francisco: Jossey-Bass.

Delgado, R., & Stefancic, J. (2012). *Critical race theory: An introduction* (2nd ed.). New York: New York University Press.

DeNavas-Walt, C., Proctor, B. D., & Smith, J. C. (2013). *Income, poverty, and health insurance coverage in the United States: 2012.* Washington, DC: U.S. Census Bureau.

Dizon, N. Z., Feller, B., & Bass, F. (2006, April 18). States omitting minorities' test scores. *Associated Press.* Accessed at www.boston .com/education/k_12/articles/2006/04/18/ap_states_omit _minorities_school_scores on October 27, 2008.

Dougherty, J., Harrelson, J., Maloney, L., Murphy, D., Smith, R., Snow, M., et al. (2009). School choice in suburbia: Test scores, race, and housing markets. *American Journal of Education, 115*(4), 523–548.

Douglass, F. (1857). *If there is no struggle, there is no progress.* In *Two speeches by Frederick Douglass.* Rochester, NY: O. P. Dewey. Accessed at www.blackpast.org/1857-frederick-douglass-if-there -no-struggle-there-no-progress on April 16, 2015.

Du Bois, W. E. B. (2008). *The souls of black folk*. Rockville, MD: Arc Manor.

Duckworth, A. L., & Eskreis-Winkler, L. (2013). True grit. *The Observer, 26*(4). Accessed at www.psychologicalscience.org /index.php/publications/observer/2013/april-13/true-grit.html on November 10, 2014.

DuFour, R., DuFour, R., & Eaker, R. (2008). *Revisiting professional learning communities at work: New insights for improving schools*. Bloomington, IN: Solution Tree Press.

DuFour, R., DuFour, R., Eaker, R., & Many, T. W. (2010). *Learning by doing: A handbook for professional learning communities at work* (2nd ed.). Bloomington, IN: Solution Tree Press.

Dweck, C. S. (2006). *Mindset: The new psychology of success*. New York: Ballantine Books.

Editorial Board. (2014, April 13). Why Michigan is so far behind others on education [Editorial]. *Detroit Free Press*. Accessed at http://archive.freep.com/article/20140413/OPINION01 /304130042/schools-standards-states-education-EdTrust -Midwest-tests-teachers on November 10, 2014.

Editorial Projects in Education Research Center. (2011). Issues A-Z: Achievement gap. *Education Week*. Accessed at www.edweek.org /ew/issues/achievement-gap on April 13, 2015.

Education for All Handicapped Children Act of 1975, 20 U.S.C. § 1401 (1975).

Egalitarianism. (n.d.). In *Merriam-Webster's collegiate dictionary* (11th ed.). Accessed at www.merriam-webster.com/dictionary /egalitarianism on January 8, 2014.

The Elementary and Secondary Education Act of 1965, as amended, 20 U.S.C. § 241 (1974).

English Language Education for Children in Public Schools, Proposition 203. (2000).

Farkas, G. (1996). *Human capital or cultural capital?: Ethnicity and poverty groups in an urban school district*. New York: de Gruyter.

Feller, B. (2006, April 19). AP poll: Teachers dubious of "No Child." *Associated Press*. Accessed at www.highbeam.com/doc/1p1-122146681 .html on October 27, 2008.

Fischer, R., Hanke, K., & Sibley, C. G. (2012). Cultural and institutional determinants of social dominance orientation: A cross-cultural meta-analysis of 27 societies. *Political Psychology, 33*(4), 437–467.

Frankenberg, E., & Orfield, G. (Eds.). (2012). *The resegregation of suburban schools: A hidden crisis in American education.* Cambridge, MA: Harvard Education Press.

Freire, P. (2000). *Pedagogy of the oppressed* (30th anniversary ed.) [M. B. Ramos, trans.]. New York: Continuum.

Fullan, M. (2003). *The moral imperative of school leadership.* Thousand Oaks, CA: Corwin Press.

Gándara, P., & Orfield, G. (2010). Moving from failure to a new vision for language policy. In P. Gándara & M. Hopkins (Eds.), *Forbidden language: English learners and restrictive language policies* (pp. 216–226). New York: Teachers College Press.

Garcia, E. E., Lawton, K., & de Figueiredo, E. H. D. (2010). *The education of English language learners in Arizona: A legacy of persisting achievement gaps in a restrictive language policy climate.* Los Angeles: The Civil Rights Project.

Gardner, H. (1995). Cracking open the IQ box. *The American Prospect, 20*, 71–80. Accessed at www.psych.utoronto.ca/users /reingold/courses/intelligence/cache/20gard.html on April 16, 2015.

Gardner, J. W. (1988). *Leadership: An overview.* Washington, DC: Leadership Studies Program, Independent Sector.

Gates, H. L., Jr. (2014, January 6). How many slaves landed in the US? *The Root*. Accessed at www.theroot.com/articles/history /2012/10/how_many_slaves_came_to_america_fact_vs_fiction .html on November 10, 2014.

Glasser, W. (1998). *Choice theory: A new psychology of personal freedom.* New York: HarperCollins.

Gonzalez-Barrera, A., Lopez, M. H., Passel, J. S., & Taylor, P. (2013). *The path not taken.* Accessed at www.pewhispanic.org/2013/02 /04/the-path-not-taken on January 7, 2015.

Gordon, J.-S. (2015). Moral egalitarianism. *Internet Encyclopedia of Philosophy.* Accessed at www.iep.utm.edu/moral-eg/#SH4a on April 16, 2015.

Gosa, T. L. (2008). *Oppositional culture, hip-hop, and the schooling of black youth.* Doctoral dissertation, Johns Hopkins University.

Gould, S. J. (1994). Curveball. *The New Yorker, 70,* 139–149.

Green, R. L. (2009). *ExpectA+ions: How teacher expectations can increase student achievement and assist in closing the achievement gap.* Columbus, OH: SRA/McGraw-Hill.

Hargreaves, S. (2013, September 17). *15% of Americans living in poverty.* Accessed at http://money.cnn.com/2013/09/17/news /economy/poverty-income on May 10, 2014.

Hattie, J. A. C. (2009). *Visible learning: A synthesis of over 800 meta-analyses relating to achievement.* New York: Routledge.

Heffner, C. L. (2002, August 21). *Personality synopsis—Section 2: Alfred Adler's individual psychology.* Accessed at http://allpsych .com/personalitysynopsis/adler.html on November 6, 2014.

Herrnstein, R. J., & Murray, C. (1994). *The bell curve: Intelligence and class structure in American life.* New York: Free Press.

Hess, F. M. (2011). Our achievement-gap mania. *National Affairs, 9.* Accessed at www.nationalaffairs.com/publications/detail/our -achievement-gap-mania on November 10, 2014.

Higgins, L., & Dawsey, C. P. (2008, April 23). Changes to No Child unveiled: Education chief—Reforms aimed at boosting nation's graduation rates. *Detroit Free Press.* Accessed at http://archive .freep.com/article/20080423/NEWS01/804230346/Changes -No-Child-unveiled on November 10, 2014.

Hoffer, E. (1951). *The true believer: Thoughts on the nature of mass movements.* New York: Harper & Row.

Horwitz, S. (2014, March 13). Holder calls for reduced sentences for low-level drug offenders. *Washington Post*. Accessed at www .washingtonpost.com/world/national-security/holder-will-call-for -reduced-sentences-for-low-level-drug-offenders/2014/03/12 /625ed9e6-aa12-11e3-8599-ce7295b6851c_story.html on November 10, 2014.

Independence Hall Association. (n.d.). *13a. The Declaration of Independence and its legacy*. Accessed at www.ushistory.org /us/13a.asp on April 30, 2014.

Individuals With Disabilities Education Act, 20 U.S.C. § 1400 (2004).

Ingraham, C. (2014). *White people are more likely to deal drugs, but blacks are more likely to get arrested for it*. Accessed at www .washingtonpost.com/blogs/wonkblog/wp/2014/09/30/white -people-are-more-likely-to-deal-drugs-but-black-people-are -more-likely-to-get-arrested-for-it on April 15, 2015.

Isensee, L., & Vasquez, M. (2012, October 13). Criticism follows Florida's race-based student achievement goals. *Miami Herald*. Accessed at www.miamiherald.com/2012/10/13/3049005 /criticism-follows-floridas-race.html on January 17, 2013.

Jackson, Y. (2011). *The pedagogy of confidence: Inspiring high intellectual performance in urban schools*. New York: Teachers College Press.

Jargowsky, P. (2013). *Concentration of poverty in the new millennium: Changes in the prevalence, composition, and location of high-poverty neighborhoods*. New York: The Center Foundation and Rutgers Center for Urban Research and Education.

Jencks, C., & Phillips, M. (Eds.). (1998). *The black–white test score gap*. Washington, DC: Brookings Institution Press.

Kentucky Department of Education. (2014). *Kentucky's school report card*. Accessed at http://applications.education.ky.gov/SRC on April 11, 2014.

Kentucky Department of Education and AdvancED. (2013). *Diagnostic review report for Seneca High School.* Louisville: Kentucky Department of Education. Accessed at http://education.ky.gov/school/documents/seneca%20dr%20report%20final%2007292013.pdf on April 13, 2015.

King, D. (1995). *Separate and unequal: Black Americans and the US federal government.* New York: Oxford University Press.

Klein, A. (2010). Debate heats up over replacing AYP metric in ESEA. *Education Week, 29*(21). Accessed at www.edweek.org/ew/articles/2010/02/05/21eseaweb_ep.h29.html on November 6, 2014.

Klein, M. H. (1951). *Self-pity: Five out of five have it.* New York: Exposition Press.

Kozol, J. (1991). *Savage inequalities: Children in American schools.* New York: Crown.

Kranich, N. (Ed.). (2001). *Libraries and democracy: The cornerstones of liberty.* Chicago: American Library Association.

Kuhnhenn, J. (2013, December 4). Obama: Income inequality is "defining challenge of our time." *Huffington Post.* Accessed at www.huffingtonpost.com/2013/12/04/obama-income-inequality_n_4384843.html on June 15, 2014.

Ladson-Billings, G. (2009). *The dreamkeepers: Successful teachers of African American children* (2nd ed.). San Francisco: Jossey-Bass.

Ladson-Billings, G., & Tate, W. F. (1995). Toward a critical race theory of education. *Teachers College Record, 97*(1), 47–68.

Langlois, J. H., Kalakanis, L., Rubenstein, A. J., Larson, A., Hallam, M., & Smoot, M. (2000). Maxims or myths of beauty? A meta-analytic and theoretical review. *Psychological Bulletin, 126*(3), 390–423.

Lareau, A., & Goyette, K. (Eds.). (2014). *Choosing homes, choosing schools: Residential segregation and the search for a good school.* New York: Russell Sage Foundation.

Lee, T. (2014). *Education racial gap as wide as ever according to NAEP*. Accessed at www.msnbc.com/msnbc/student-proficiency-stagnant-race-gap-wide on April 15, 2015.

Levin, S., Federico, C. M., Sidanius, J., & Rabinowitz, J. L. (2002). Social dominance orientation and intergroup bias: The legitimation of favoritism for high-status groups. *Personality and Social Psychology Bulletin, 28*(2), 144–157.

Lewis, B. (n.d.). *Martin Luther King's "I Have a Dream" speech: Address at March on Washington for Jobs and Freedom*. Accessed at http://k6educators.about.com/cs/martinlutherking/a/mlkspeech.htm on November 10, 2014.

Lewis, O. (1998). The culture of poverty. *Society, 35*(2), 7–9.

Lezotte, L. W. (2001). *Revolutionary and evolutionary: The Effective Schools movement*. Okemos, MI: Effective Schools Products.

Lilley, S. (2012). *Poll: 1 out of 3 Americans inaccurately think that most Hispanics are undocumented*. Accessed at http://nbclatino.com/2012/09/12/poll-1-out-of-3-americans-think-most-hispanics-are-undocumented on April 15, 2015.

Lippmann, W. (1922). *Public opinion*. New York: Harcourt, Brace.

Lloyd, S. A., & Sreedhar, S. (2014). Hobbes's moral and political philosophy. In Edward N. Zalta (Ed.), *The Stanford Encyclopedia of Philosophy* (Spring 2014 Edition). Accessed at http://plato.stanford.edu/archives/spr2014/entries/hobbes-moral on April 13, 2015.

Lortie, D. C. (1975). *Schoolteacher: A sociological study*. Chicago: University of Chicago Press.

Lyons, P. A., Coursey, L. E., & Kenworthy, J. B. (2013). National identity and group narcissism as predictors of intergroup attitudes toward undocumented Latino immigrants in the United States. *Hispanic Journal of Behavioral Sciences, 35*(3), 323–335.

Mahoney, K., MacSwan, J., Haladyna, T., & Garcia, D. (2010). Castaneda's third prong: Evaluating the achievement of Arizona's English learners under restrictive language policy. In P. Gándara & M. Hopkins (Eds.), *Forbidden language: English learners and restrictive language policies* (pp. 50–64). New York: Teachers College Press.

Marshall, G. (1998). Functional inequality. *A Dictionary of Sociology.* Accessed at www.encyclopedia.com/doc/1O88-functional -inequality.html on November 10, 2014.

Martin Luther King Jr. Elementary School. (2014). *School accountability report card: Dynamic 2014–15 report.* Accessed at www.axiomadvisors.net/livesarc/Presentation/MainPortal.aspx ?CDS=16639176113609&LanguageID=1&Preview=False on March 15, 2014.

Marzano, R. J. (2003). *What works in schools: Translating research into action.* Alexandria, VA: Association for Supervision and Curriculum Development.

Mauer, M. (2006). *Race to incarcerate* (Rev. and 2nd ed.). New York: New Press.

McIntyre, J. (2008, September 3). The soft bigotry of low expectations. *Daily Kos.* Accessed at www.dailykos.com/story/2008/09 /03/584487/-The-Soft-Bigotry-of-Low-Expectations# on September 3, 2008.

Melago, C. (2008, February 3). Left in dark over No Child Left Behind. *New York Daily News.* Accessed at www.nydailynews .com/new-york/education/left-dark-child-left-behind-article -1.306014 on November 10, 2014.

Melchior, J. K. (2013, December 12). Michigan teachers locked in. *National Review.* Accessed at www.nationalreview.com/article /366117/michigan-teachers-locked-jillian-kay-melchior on November 10, 2014.

Meritocracy. (n.d.). In *Merriam-Webster's collegiate dictionary* (11th ed.). Accessed at www.merriam-webster.com/dictionary /egalitarianism on January 8, 2014.

Michigan Department of Education. (2014). *Michigan's school accreditation system: Education Yes!* Accessed at www.michigan .gov/mde/0,1607,7-140-5234_5704-24878--,00.html on May 10, 2014.

Morse, A. (2011). *Arizona's immigration enforcement laws.* Accessed at www.ncsl.org/research/immigration/analysis-of-arizonas -immigration-law.aspx on May 5, 2014.

Mosak, H. H., & Maniacci, M. P. (1999). *A primer of Adlerian psychology: The analytic-behavioral-cognitive psychology of Alfred Adler.* New York: Brunner/Mazel.

Muhammad, A. (2009). *Transforming school culture: How to overcome staff division.* Bloomington, IN: Solution Tree Press.

Muhammad, A., & Hollie, S. (2012). *The will to lead, the skill to teach: Transforming schools at every level.* Bloomington, IN: Solution Tree Press.

No Child Left Behind Act of 2001, Pub. L. No. 107–110, § 115, Stat. 1425 (2002).

Office of Applied Studies, Substance Abuse and Mental Health Services Administration. (2001). *Summary of findings from the 2000 National Household Survey on Drug Abuse* (DHHS Publication No. SMA 01–3549, NHSDA Series H-13). Rockville, MD: Author.

Ogbu, J. U. (2003). *Black American students in an affluent suburb: A study of academic disengagement.* Mahwah, NJ: Erlbaum.

Orr, J. (2009, October 14). Our top ten favorite John Wooden quotes. *Christian Science Monitor.* Accessed at www.csmonitor.com /USA/Politics/The-Vote/2009/1014/our-top-ten-favorite-john -wooden-quotes on November 10, 2014.

Pasek, J., Krosnik, J. A., & Tompson, T. (2012). *The impact of anti- black racism on approval of Barack Obama's job performance and on voting in the 2012 presidential election.* Stanford, CA: Stanford University.

Passel, J. S., Cohn, D., & Lopez, M. H. (2011). *Hispanics account for more than half of the nation's growth in the past decade.* Accessed at www.pewhispanic.org/2011/03/24/hispanics-account-for-more -than-half-of-nations-growth-in-past-decade on January 7, 2015.

Pavao, E. (2014). *Slavery and the founding fathers.* Accessed at www .revolutionary-war.net/slavery-and-the-founding-fathers.html on April 30, 2014.

Peterson, P. E., & Hess, F. (2008). Few states set world-class standards: In fact, most render the notion of proficiency meaningless. *Education Next, 8*(3), 70–73.

Petrides, L., & Nodine, T. (2005). *Anatomy of school system improvement: Performance-driven practices in urban school districts.* Half Moon Bay, CA: Institute for the Study of Knowledge Management in Education.

Pew Hispanic Center. (2002). *U.S. born Hispanics increasingly drive population developments.* Accessed at www.pewhispanic.org/2002 /01/01/u-s-born-hispanics-increasingly-drive-population -developments on January 7, 2015.

Pew Research Center for the People and the Press. (2012, January 23). *Public priorities: Deficit rising, terrorism slipping—Tough stance on Iran endorsed.* Accessed at www.people-press.org /2012/01/23/public-priorities-deficit-rising-terrorism-slipping on January 15, 2014.

Pfeffer, J., & Sutton, R. (2000). *The knowing-doing gap: How smart companies turn knowledge into action.* Cambridge, MA: Harvard Business School Press.

Planas, R. (2013, March 11). Arizona's law banning Mexican-American studies curriculum is constitutional, judge rules. *Huffington Post.* Accessed at www.huffingtonpost.com/2013 /03/11/arizona-mexican-american-studies-curriculum -constitutional_n_2851034.html on May 5, 2014.

Popova, M. (n.d.). *Fixed vs. growth: The two basic mindsets that shape our lives.* Accessed at www.brainpickings.org/2014/01/29/carol -dweck-mindset on April 13, 2015.

Proposition 203 (2000), 6A Ariz. Stat. Ann. § § 15-751-755

Racism. (n.d.). In *Merriam-Webster's collegiate dictionary* (11th ed.). Accessed at www.merriam-webster.com/dictionary/racism on January 8, 2014.

Ravitch, D. (2013). *Reign of error: The hoax of the privatization movement and the danger to America's public schools.* New York: Vintage Books.

Recovery.org. (2014). *Finding the best 12-step substance abuse recovery programs.* Accessed at www.recovery.org/topics/12-step -substance-abuse-recovery-programs on April 30, 2014.

Roberts, J. V., & Hough, M. (Eds.). (2002). *Changing attitudes to punishment: Public opinion, crime and justice.* Portland, OR: Willan.

Rodriguez, R. C. (2012, July 16). The face of "reasonable suspicion": Arizona's freedom summer continues. *Truthout.* Accessed at http://truth-out.org/opinion/item/10355-the-face-of-%E2%80 %9Creasonable-suspicion%E2%80%9D-arizona%E2%80%99s -freedom-summer-continues on May 5, 2014.

Roosevelt, E. (2001). *My day: The best of Eleanor Roosevelt's acclaimed newspaper columns, 1936–1962* (D. Emblidge, Ed.). Cambridge, MA: Da Capo Press.

Ruiz, D. M. (1997). *The four agreements: A practical guide to personal freedom.* San Rafael, CA: Amber-Allen.

S. 2281, 49th Cong. § 15-112 (2010). Accessed at www.azleg.gov /legtext/49leg/2r/bills/hb2281s.pdf on January 7, 2015.

Sadovi, C., Malone, T., & Black, L. (2008, September 3). Chicago public school students skip class in show of activism. *Chicago Tribune.* Accessed at http://articles.chicagotribune.com/2008-09 -03/news/0809020867_1_sen-james-meeks-chicago-public -school-students-chicago-mercantile-exchange on November 10, 2014.

Santiago, B. (2011). King Elementary makes strides with English learner curriculum. *Hanford Sentinel.* Accessed at http://hanfordsentinel.com/news/local/king-elementary-makes-strides-with-english-learner-curriculum/article_e498a8fa-1145-11e1-a26a-001cc4c002e0.html on April 13, 2015.

Schement, J. R. (2001). Imagining fairness: Equality and equity of access in search of democracy. In N. Kranich (Ed.), *Libraries & democracy: The cornerstones of liberty* (pp. 15–27). Chicago: American Library Association.

Science Encyclopedia. (n.d.). *Humor-superiority theory.* Accessed at http://science.jrank.org/pages/9715/Humor-Superiority-Theory.html on June 15, 2014.

Seligman, M. E. P. (1975). *Helplessness: On depression, development, and death.* San Francisco: Freeman.

Seneca High School. (n.d.). *Seneca specifics.* Accessed at www.jefferson.k12.ky.us/schools/high/Seneca/senecaspecifics.html on December 3, 2014.

Shaw, B. (2008, March 12). Our nation still at risk. *Education Week, 27*(27).

Sidanius, J., & Pratto, F. (1999). *Social dominance: An intergroup theory of social hierarchy and oppression.* New York: Cambridge University Press.

Siegel, H. (2011, December 16). Education tour partner Al Sharpton doesn't back Newt Gingrich's reforms. *Daily Beast.* Accessed at www.thedailybeast.com/articles/2011/12/16/education-tour-partner-al-sharpton-doesn-t-back-newt-gingrich-s-reforms.html on November 10, 2014.

Singleton, G. E. (1997). *White is a color!* Paper presented at the National Summit for Courageous Conversation of the Pacific Educational Group, San Francisco.

Singleton, G. E., & Linton, C. (2006). *Courageous conversations about race: A field guide for achieving equity in schools.* Thousand Oaks, CA: Corwin Press.

Sisk, R. (2009, May 16). Newt Gingrich and Al Sharpton team up to rally for education tour. *New York Daily News*. Accessed at www .nydailynews.com/news/politics/newt-gingrich-al-sharpton-team -rally-education-tour-article-1.413138 on November 6, 2014.

Snyder, J., Brooker, M., Patrick, M. R., Snyder, A., Schrepferman, L., & Stoolmiller, M. (2003). Observed peer victimization during early elementary school: Continuity, growth, and relation to risk for child antisocial and depressive behavior. *Child Development*, *74*(6), 1881–1898.

Stafford, M. (1989). *W.E.B. Du Bois: Scholar and activist*. New York: Chelsea.

Stake, R. E. (1991). The teacher, standardized testing, and prospects of revolution. *Phi Delta Kappan*, *73*(3), 243–247.

Stipek, D. J. (1988). *Motivation to learn: From theory to practice*. Boston: Allyn & Bacon.

Stöber, J. (2003). Self-pity: Exploring the links to personality, control beliefs, and anger. *Journal of Personality*, *71*(2), 183–220.

Strauss, V. (2013, November 16). Arne Duncan: "White suburban moms" upset that Common Core shows their kids aren't "brilliant" [Web log post]. *The Washington Post*. Accessed at www .washingtonpost.com/blogs/answer-sheet/wp/2013/11/16/arne -duncan-white-surburban-moms-upset-that-common-core-shows -their-kids-arent-brilliant on November 6, 2014.

Sullivan, D. R., Liu, X., Corwin, D. S., Verceles, A. C., McCurdy, M. T., Pate, D. A., et al. (2012). Learned helplessness among families and surrogate decision-makers of patients admitted to medical, surgical, and trauma ICUs. *Chest*, *142*(6), 1440–1446.

Support Our Law Enforcement and Safe Neighborhoods Act of 2010, 4-5C Ariz. Stat. Ann. § § 13-101-3801

Tauber, R. T. (1998). Good or bad, what teachers expect from students they generally get! *ERIC Digest* (ED426985). Accessed at http://files.eric.ed.gov/fulltext/ED426985.pdf on November 6, 2014.

Thernstrom, A., & Thernstrom, S. (2003). *No excuses: Closing the racial gap in learning.* New York: Simon & Schuster.

Therrien, M., & Ramirez, R. R. (2001). *The Hispanic population in the United States: Population characteristics, March 2000* (Current Population Reports, P20–535). Washington, DC: U.S. Census Bureau.

Thompson, D. (Ed.). (2001). *The essential E. P. Thompson.* New York: New Press.

Toppo, G. (2008, May 2). Study: Reading First has little impact on kids' scores. *USA Today*, 4A.

Trumbul, E., Rothstein-Fisch, C., & Greenfield, P. M. (2000). *Bridging cultures in our schools: New approaches that work* (Knowledge Brief). San Francisco: WestEd.

Tyack, D., & Cuban, L. (1995). *Tinkering toward utopia: A century of public school reform.* Cambridge, MA: Harvard University Press.

U.S. Census Bureau. (2014). *Facts for features: Hispanic Heritage Month 2014: September 15–October 15.* Accessed at www.census .gov/newsroom/facts-for-features/2014/cb14-ff22.html on April 13, 2014.

U.S. Department of Education. (2013, August 29). *States granted waivers from No Child Left Behind allowed to reapply for renewal for 2014 and 2015 school years.* Accessed at www.ed.gov/news /press-releases/states-granted-waivers-no-child-left-behind -allowed-reapply-renewal-2014-and-201 on May 10, 2014.

U.S. Department of Education, Office for Civil Rights. (2014). *Civil rights data collection: Data snapshot—School discipline* (Issue Brief No. 1). Washington, DC: Author.

Usdan, M., McCloud, B., & Podmostko, M. (2000). *Leadership for student learning: Reinventing the principalship.* Washington, DC: Institute for Educational Leadership.

Viadero, D. (2008). Teachers advised to "get real" on race. *Education Week, 27*(21). Accessed at www.edweek.org/ew/articles/2008/01 /30/21race.h27.html on November 6, 2014.

Viadero, D. (2010). Study finds wide achievement gaps for top students. *Education Week, 29*(21). Accessed at www.edweek.org/ew/articles/2010/02/05/21gap.h29.html on November 6, 2014.

Wells, A. S., & Roda, A. (2009). *White parents, diversity and school choice policies: Where good intentions, anxiety and privilege collide.* Nashville, TN: Vanderbilt University, National Center on School Choice.

Wilson, B. L., & Corbett, H. D. (2001). *Listening to urban kids: School reform and the teachers they want.* Albany: State University of New York Press.

Wilson, W. J. (1987). *The truly disadvantaged: The inner city, the underclass, and public policy.* Chicago: University of Chicago Press.

Winerip, M. (2007, December 9). In gaps at school, weighing family life. *The New York Times.* Accessed at www.nytimes.com/2007/12/09/nyregion/nyregionspecial2/09Rparenting.html?pagewanted=all on November 6, 2014.

Zeichner K., & Gore, J. (n.d.). *Teacher socialization.* Accessed at http://ncrtl.msu.edu/http/ipapers/html/pdf/ip897.pdf on April 15, 2015.

Zuckerbrod, N. (2007, November 22). City schools gain, yet still lag nation. *Associated Press.* Accessed at http://usatoday30.usatoday.com/news/education/2007-11-15-city-schools_n.htm on January 19, 2015.

Index

A

abolitionist movement, 21–22
accountability ratings, 48–49
Achievement Gap Educational Foundation, 33
Achievement Gap Initiative (AGI), 13–14
achievement gaps
    approaches to, xviii
    defined, 13–14
    past attempts to close, 33–35
    statistics, 14–15
achievement gap trap
    defined, 10
    functional hypocrisy and inequality, 40–49
acting white, 73
activism, role of, 7–8
Adams, J., 51
adequate yearly progress (AYP), 47–48
Adler, A., 64–65, 66, 71, 79–80
advocacy, liberation mindset, 94, 104–108
African Americans
    cognitive support, 81–82
    emotional support, 82
    out-of-school assignments, 82–83
    public opinion, 17
    racism, historical overview, 21–26
    television watching, 83
Alexander, M., 22–23
apprenticeship of observation, 43
Arciniega, T., 68
Arizona, 27–30
Asian students, 16–17, 83
authority, 66, 71–74

B

Believers, 56, 58–59
Bell Curve, The (Herrnstein and Murray), 44
Berlin, I., 92
Bloom, B., xiii–xiv
Bowles, S., 32
Brainwashed: Challenging the Myth of Black Inferiority (Burrell), 25
Brewer, J., 27

T

W

Transforming School Culture
Anthony Muhammad

Busy administrators will appreciate this quick read packed with immediate, accessible strategies. This book provides the framework for understanding dynamic relationships within a school culture and ensuring a positive environment that supports the changes necessary to improve learning for all students.
BKF281

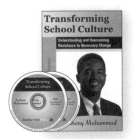

Transforming School Culture
Anthony Muhammad

Muhammad describes the prevailing beliefs and assumptions of four different types of educators: Believers, Fundamentalists, Tweeners, and Survivors. After arguing that their collective dynamic ultimately determines the culture of a school, he provides specific strategies for working with each group.
DVF022

The Will to Lead, the Skill to Teach
Anthony Muhammad, Sharroky Hollie

The authors acknowledge both the structural and sociological issues that contribute to low-performing schools and offer multiple tools and strategies to assess and improve classroom management, increase literacy, establish academic vocabulary, and contribute to a healthier school culture.
BKF443

Working With Difficult & Resistant Staff
John F. Eller, Sheila A. Eller

Identify, confront, and manage all of the difficult and resistant staff you encounter. This book will help school leaders understand how to prevent and address negative staff behaviors to ensure positive school change.
BKF407

Solution Tree | Press   *a division of*
Solution Tree

Visit solution-tree.com or call 800.733.6786 to order.

Wait! Your professional development journey doesn't have to end with the last pages of this book.

We realize improving student learning doesn't happen overnight. And your school or district shouldn't be left to puzzle out.all the details of this process alone.

No matter where you are on the journey, we're committed to helping you get to the next stage.

Take advantage of everything from **custom workshops** to **keynote presentations** and **interactive web and video conferencing**. We can even help you develop an action plan tailored to fit your specific needs.

Let's get the conversation started.

Call 888.763.9045 today.

solution-tree.com